The
Reference Shelf®

U.S. National Debate Topic 2009–2010

Social Services for the Poor

Edited by Margaret Roush

The Reference Shelf
Volume 81 • Number 3
The H.W. Wilson Company
New York • Dublin
2009

The Reference Shelf

The books in this series contain reprints of articles, excerpts from books, addresses on current issues, and studies of social trends in the United States and other countries. There are six separately bound numbers in each volume, all of which are usually published in the same calendar year. Numbers one through five are each devoted to a single subject, providing background information and discussion from various points of view and concluding with a subject index and comprehensive bibliography that lists books, pamphlets, and abstracts of additional articles on the subject. The final number of each volume is a collection of recent speeches, and it contains a cumulative speaker index. Books in the series may be purchased individually or on subscription.

Library of Congress has cataloged this serial title as follows:

U.S. national debate topic 2009-2010 : social services for the poor / edited by Margaret Roush.
    p. cm.—(The reference shelf ; v. 81, no. 3)
  Includes bibliographical references and index.
  ISBN 978-0-8242-1090-8 (alk. paper)
  1. Public welfare—United States. 2. Poor—Services for—United States. I. Roush, Margaret. II. Title: Social services for the poor.
  HV95.U25 2009
  362.5′5650973—dc22

                                      2009015310

Cover: Rural residents wait for donated food and drinks at an aid distribution site March 5, 2009 in Hugo, Colorado. Eastern Colorado has been hit hard by the recession, as the agricultural economy was already in trouble due to more than a decade of drought. The Care and Share food bank trucks food to the rural community once a month to aid a growing number of residents in need. Credit: Photo by John Moore/Getty Images

Visit H.W. Wilson's Web site: www.hwwilson.com

Printed in the United States of America

6/09

Contents

Preface

The United States is one of the only industrialized nations that does not provide a comprehensive social welfare system for its citizens. Unlike countries in Western Europe and Scandinavia, which offer a so-called "safety net" of state-supported social services, the United States by comparison spends a much lower percentage of its gross domestic product on social welfare programs, even though its poverty rate consistently ranks highest among developed nations. A primary reason for this difference has to do with culture. Unlike Europeans, who generally see poverty as an inevitable byproduct of capitalism, Americans have historically viewed poverty as the result of individual rather than institutional failure, a perspective likely shaped by the cultural values of work, individualism, and freedom of opportunity. In the 20th century, some forms of state-supported social programs gained widespread acceptance—particularly those for the elderly and retired, in the forms of Social Security benefits and Medicare. But whether and to what extent the government should provide social programs for the poor has been, and continues to be, fiercely debated questions among policymakers.

Prior to the Great Depression, caring for the poor was almost exclusively the responsibility of private institutions and state and local governments. In the 1930s the widespread poverty wrought by the Great Depression shifted the dominant ideas about the federal government's responsibility for the economic security of its citizens. No longer was poverty relegated to a small, destitute portion of the population; rather it was recognized as a hardship that could affect anyone, even members of the middle class. As part of the stimulus and economic-planning programs of the New Deal, in 1935, President Franklin D. Roosevelt signed the Social Security Act, which, in addition to offering services for the elderly and disabled, established aid programs for the poor. Among the most important was the first federally funded cash welfare system, known as Aid to Dependent Children. (That name was changed to Aid to Families with Dependent Children in 1960 due to concern that it discouraged parents from marrying.) Another enduring legacy from the Great Depression is the U.S. Housing Act, passed in 1937, which provides federal subsidies to local public housing agencies. After the economic woes of the Great Depression subsided, social programs for the poor remained a small but significant part of the federal government.

Another massive shift in social policy took place in 1964, when Democratic president Lyndon B. Johnson announced his intention to eradicate poverty and discrimination in the country and build a "Great Society." As part of his "War on Poverty," Johnson passed the Economic Opportunity Act, which established a vast array of federally funded social welfare programs aimed at providing services to the poor and expanding those programs already in existence. A number of these initiatives still exist today, including Head Start, the early education, health, nutrition, and parenting program for low-income families; Medicaid, the need-based state-run health insurance; and the Food Stamp Program, which allowed low-income citizens to obtain food. Despite the fact that poverty rates dropped over the next decade, Johnson's programs became the target of much criticism from conservative economists and politicians for greatly expanding government spending while creating what many perceived as a culture of dependency and illegitimacy among the nation's poor. Republican president Richard Nixon did much to expand some social programs, establishing Supplemental Security Income benefits for the poor and disabled, and lifting the purchase requirement from food stamp benefits, as did Jimmy Carter. On the other hand, Ronald Reagan sought to dismantle Johnson's Great Society programs during his two terms as president. Reagan summed up his views on government's proper role in social programs in his 1988 State of the Union Address, when he declared: "My friends, some years ago, the federal government declared a war on poverty—and poverty won."

President Bill Clinton's 1996 Personal Responsibility and Work Reconciliation Act (PRWRA) amounted to a monumental change in the nation's social policy toward the poor. Containing the welfare reform bill, Temporary Assistance to Needy Families (TANF), the legislation reduced funding to social programs across the board and introduced additional regulations that incentivized work. Coupled with the expanding 1990s economy, the controversial legislation led to decreased rates of welfare participation, unemployment, and child poverty, and was widely-praised by members of both parties. Indeed, some even declared the problem of poverty solved. In 2000, however, the economic situation changed, and over the next several years, poverty rates began to creep higher, along with figures for unemployed adults, homeless families, and children lacking health insurance. President George W. Bush did little to expand the government's role in the social welfare of the poor. He passed the 2005 Deficit Reduction Act, which placed additional regulations on many social programs, particularly Medicaid, and vetoed two bills that would have greatly expanded the State Children's Health Insurance Plan (SCHIP), a program created in 1997 to insure low-income children who did not qualify for Medicaid.

Today, in 2009, the country's social policies are at a crossroads. Faced with a deep and troubling economic recession and rising unemployment, many of the social welfare systems in place do not seem to be holding up. Given the depth of the economic crisis, the scope of President Obama's recent proposals, and the degree of his popular support, there is little doubt that the Obama presidency will usher in a new era of expanded government programs for the poor. In February 2009 President Obama signed into law the American Recovery and Reinvestment Act, a spending bill worth close to $800 billion, aimed at funding projects and creating jobs to stimulate the economy. The act allocated $82.5 billion in aid to low-income workers, retirees, and the unemployed through job-training and employment services, unemployment insurance, food stamp benefits, and other programs. As of this writing President Obama has also presented a massive 10-year, $3.6 trillion budget to Congress, which includes significant increases in social welfare expenditures.

The larger question, however, is this: Will Obama do more than expand the existing need-based programs and accomplish the goal that has so far eluded progressives—the creation of a true social safety net, one that offers a coherent set of programs mandating and implementing universal health insurance, affordable childcare, a living wage, etc., that makes the high poverty and inequality rates in the United States a thing of the past? The answer to this question remains to be seen.

This book is divided into five chapters. The first, "'Water, Water Everywhere': Perspectives on Poverty and in the United States," contains five articles that examine in a general sense the relationships between poverty and policy in the United States. The arguments in each piece are shaped to varying degrees by the political bent of the writers, offering a vigorous introduction to the topic of poverty. The selections in the second section, "Welfare Since Reform: Is It Still Relevant?," chart the wide-ranging effects of Clinton's 1996 reforms on U.S. welfare policy. Each article discusses whether welfare reform was "successful" and examines the program's role in the present day. Pieces in the third chapter, "The Medicaid and SCHIP Debates," cover the many relevant perspectives surrounding the reform and expansion of the government's two principle need-based insurance programs. The fourth section, "Feeding America's Hungry: Food Stamps/Supplemental Nutrition Assistance," includes selections that chart the history of the nation's largest hunger-relief program and examine the perplexing problem of hunger in the United States. The fifth chapter contains articles addressing other pertinent aspects of poverty, related to the previous three, including low-income housing, disability, and early childhood education.

Margaret Roush
June 2009

1

"Water, Water Everywhere":
Perspectives on Poverty in the United States

Editor's Introduction

Much ado was made when rates of poverty, unemployment, and enrollment in federally funded social programs in the United States began to fall in the late 1990s after decades of the opposite trend. Many found at least some explanation in the booming economy of the 1990s. Many others attributed the falling rates to the sweeping social policy reforms enacted by President Bill Clinton's Personal Responsibility and Work Reconciliation Act (PRWRA). Aimed at curbing the entitlement programs established during President Lyndon Johnson's "War on Poverty" and instilling in the poor a sense of personal responsibility and a bootstraps-style work ethic, the theme of PRWRA was exemplified by its welfare reform provision, Temporary Assistance for Needy Families (TANF), which replaced the former entitlement program, Aid to Families with Dependent Children (AFDC), with a system that, among other changes, linked cash benefits to work requirements and placed limitations on the length of time a family could collect benefits. Proponents claimed that these and other small government "bottom-up" policies championed in the 1990s led to higher employment and lower poverty rates by changing the system of incentives and eliminating a "culture of dependency." Whatever the reason, by 2000, poverty and unemployment had sunk to record lows and politicians appeared to have closed the book on the subject. As talk of terrorism and homeland security came to dominate the national debate in 2001, the plight of the poor effectively drifted from the public consciousness.

In President George W. Bush's first term, the issue of poverty continued to recede from public awareness, overshadowed by the War on Terror, the Iraq War, and other issues. During the 2004 election campaign, Democratic presidential aspirant and eventual vice presidential-nominee John Edwards spoke often about poverty, but the conventional wisdom that says the poor don't elect the president prevailed, and the country continued to look the other way. Meanwhile, increasing numbers of the poor were working full-time, low-paying jobs that lacked benefits and health insurance. However, Hurricane Katrina, which devastated New Orleans, Louisiana, and the surrounding Gulf Coast in August 2005, caused the issue to resurface and made it once again a topic of national debate. In New Orleans the storm reduced a largely impoverished population to utter destitution. As the images of abject hopelessness entered American living rooms, people could not ignore that extreme poverty was indeed prevalent in America's less visible communities. Bush resolved to tackle the problem, declaring, "We have a duty to confront this poverty with bold action. So let us restore all that we have cherished from yesterday, and let us rise above the legacy of inequality." The reforms contained in the 2005 Deficit Reduction Act, however, did little to change the course of President Clinton's conservative reforms. Rather, the act was designed to accelerate the reduction of welfare recipients and cut the size of the overall program.

Around the same time that the public dismissed poverty as an urgent problem, in 2000, studies show that poverty actually began to increase. And as welfare enrollment steadily declined, the poor were signing up for programs such as Medicaid, food stamps, disability benefits, and unemployment payments in record numbers. Despite TANF's focus on reducing its enrollment, that initiative too has recently seen an uptick, for which many state governments are unprepared. Today, in the thick of an economic recession and record job losses, President Barack Obama has set forth a bold plan to make poverty a national priority. His 2009 budget aims to considerably increase funding for existing social programs, and Obama has expressed his intention to overhaul other systems, most notably that of health care, which may lead to dramatic changes in the way we look at poverty.

The articles contained in this section examine the relationships between poverty and policy in the United States. In the first piece, "The Other America," Jonathan Alter discusses the impact of Hurricane Katrina, and the systemic poverty it revealed in New Orleans and the surrounding Gulf communities, on the country's perspective on the lives of its poor. While acknowledging the accomplishments of such programs as Social Security and Medicare, and reforms such as the Earned Income Tax Credit and TANF, Alter also asserts that poverty has gotten worse since the end of the 1990s as a result of a complex combination of culture, racism, isolation, policy, and low wages. William E. Spriggs, in the subsequent piece, "The Changing Face of Poverty in America," suggests that poverty is the direct result of policy choices that view different groups—children, the disabled, the elderly, and the unemployed—as more or less deserving of aid.

Taking a conservative perspective, Jeffrey M. Jones, in "Poverty Row," discusses the rhetoric of several of the 2008 presidential candidates on the issue of poverty. He compares the views of John Edwards and Republican senator Sam Brownback and argues that Brownback's market-based solutions are more constructive. Providing a vivid counterpoint to Jones' piece, Ezra Klein, in "Poverty Is Back!" offers a primer on how Hurricane Katrina transformed American thinking on poverty and provides "a rough synthesis of progressive policy solutions to poverty." In the final piece, "We Don't Need Another War On Poverty," Steven Malanga disparages then-Senator Barack Obama's plans to stimulate the U.S. economy by using federal money to fund public schools, housing, job training, and social-welfare programs as stale, wasteful reenactments of Johnson's "War on Poverty" measures. Malanga advocates the local strategies used in the 1990s to address social woes, including funding for local law enforcement and school vouchers.

The Other America*

By Jonathan Alter
Newsweek, September 19, 2005

It takes a hurricane. It takes a catastrophe like Katrina to strip away the old evasions, hypocrisies and not-so-benign neglect. It takes the sight of the United States with a big black eye—visible around the world—to help the rest of us begin to see again. For the moment, at least, Americans are ready to fix their restless gaze on enduring problems of poverty, race and class that have escaped their attention. Does this mean a new war on poverty? No, especially with Katrina's garagantuan price tag. But this disaster may offer a chance to start a skirmish, or at least make Washington think harder about why part of the richest country on earth looks like the Third World.

"I hope we realize that the people of New Orleans weren't just abandoned during the hurricane," Sen. Barack Obama said last week on the floor of the Senate. "They were abandoned long ago—to murder and mayhem in the streets, to substandard schools, to dilapidated housing, to inadequate health care, to a pervasive sense of hopelessness."

The question now is whether the floodwaters can create a sea change in public perceptions. "Americans tend to think of poor people as being responsible for their own economic woes," says sociologist Andrew Cherlin of Johns Hopkins University. "But this was a case where the poor were clearly not at fault. It was a reminder that we have a moral obligation to provide every American with a decent life."

In the last four decades, part of that obligation has been met. Social Security and Medicare have all but eliminated poverty among the elderly. Food stamps have made severe hunger in the United States mostly a thing of the past. A little-known program with bipartisan support and a boring name—the Earned Income Tax Credit—supplements the puny wages of the working poor, helping to lift millions into the lower middle class.

But after a decade of improvement in the 1990s, poverty in America is actually getting worse. A rising tide of economic growth is no longer lifting all boats. For the first time in half a century, the third year of a recovery (2004) also saw an increase in poverty. In a nation of nearly 300 million people, the number living below the poverty line ($14,680 for a family of three) recently hit 37 million, up more than a million in a year. With the strain Katrina is placing on the gulf region (and on families putting up their displaced relatives), it will almost certainly increase more.

The poverty rate, 12.7 percent, is a controversial measurement, in part because it doesn't include some supplemental programs. But it's the highest in the developed world and more than twice as high as in most other industrialized countries, which all strike a more generous social contract with their weakest citizens. Even if the real number is lower than 37 million, that's a nation of poor people the size of Canada or Morocco living inside the United States.

Their fellow Americans know little about them. In the last decade, poverty disappeared from public view. TV dislikes poor people, not personally but because their appearance is a downer and—according to ratings meters—causes viewers to hit the remote. Powerful politicians aren't much friendlier: poor folks vote in small numbers. Republicans win little of their support and Democrats often take it for granted.

Until Katrina, the pressure was off. After President Clinton signed welfare reform in 1996, the chattering classes stopped arguing about it. With welfare case loads cut in half—more than 9 million women and children have left the rolls— even many liberals figured the trend lines were headed in the right direction. The real-world challenges of welfare reform explained in Jason DeParle's landmark 2004 book, "American Dream," went unheeded, as Clinton initiatives and the boom of the 1990s pulled 4.1 million of the working poor out of poverty. (Good times don't always have that effect. The Reagan boom of the 1980s did the same for only 50,000.) Meanwhile crime plummeted in cities across the country, down to levels not seen since the 1950s. Few noticed that progress in fighting poverty stalled with the economy in 2001.

President Bush, preoccupied with terrorism and tax cuts, made no mention of it. His main involvement with poverty issues has been on education, where he sharply increased aid to poor schools as part of his No Child Left Behind initiative. Democrats have offered little on education beyond opposition to NCLB. They've shown more allegiance to the teachers unions (whose contracts are models of unaccountability) than to poor kids. Bush's other antipoverty idea was to bolster so-called faith-based initiatives by shifting a little federal funding of social programs to religious groups. Post-Katrina, this will likely be extended. But it's a Band-Aid, not an antipoverty strategy. The last notable poverty expert working in the White House, John Dilulio, departed in 2001 after explaining that the administration had no interest in real policy analysis.

The president has made a point of hiring more high-ranking African-Americans than any of his predecessors. But his identification with blacks is a long way

from, say, LBJ's intoning, as he did in 1965, "Their cause must be our cause, too
. . . And we shall overcome." Bush rarely meets with the poor or their representatives. His mother made headlines when she visited the Houston Astrodome and
said: "So many of the people in the arenas here, you know, were underprivileged
anyway. So this is working very well for them"—as if sharing space with 10,000
strangers was a step up.

Who are the poor? With whites making up 72 percent of the population, the
United States contains more poor whites than poor blacks or Hispanics. In fact,
the Center on Budget and Policy Priorities reports that the increase in white poverty in nonurban areas accounts for most of the recent uptick in the poverty rate.
But only a little more than 8 percent of American whites are poor, compared
with 22 percent of Hispanics and nearly a quarter of all African-Americans (in a
country that is 12 percent black). This represents a significant advance for blacks
in recent decades, thanks to the growth of the black middle class, but it's still a
shamefully high number. By contrast, immigration has sent poverty among Hispanics up, though it has not been as intractable for them across generations.

After 40 years of study, the causes of poverty are still being debated. Liberals say the problem is an economic system that's tilted to the rich; conservatives
blame a debilitating culture of poverty. Clearly, it's both—a tangle of financial and
personal pain that often goes beyond insufficient resources and lack of training.
Family issues are critical, married-couple families are significantly less poor than
female-headed households. While hunger, crime, drugs and overt racial discrimination have eased, other problems connected with poverty may have worsened:
wage stagnation, social isolation and a more subtle form of class-based racism.
Each can be found in New Orleans, pre-Katrina.

The primary economic problem is not unemployment but low wages for workers of all races. With unions weakened and a minimum-wage increase not on
the GOP agenda, wages have not kept pace with the cost of living, except at
the top. (In 1965, CEOs made 24 times as much as the average worker; by 2003,
they earned 185 times as much.) Since 2001, the United States has lost 2.7 million manufacturing jobs. New Orleans's good jobs left much earlier, replaced by
employment in the restaurant and tourism industry, which pays less and usually
carries no health benefits. Medicaid covers poor children but few poor adults, who
put off seeing the doctor, cranking up the cost. For the poor, the idea of low-wage
jobs covering the basic expenses of living has become a cruel joke.

Consider the case of Delores Ellis. Before Katrina turned her world upside
down, the 51-year-old resident of New Orleans's Ninth Ward was earning the
highest salary of her life as a school janitor—$6.50 an hour, no health insurance
or pension. Pregnant at 17 and forced to drop out of high school, she went on
welfare for a time, then bounced around minimum-wage jobs. "I worked hard all
my life and I can't afford nothing," Ellis says. "I'm not saying that I want to keep
up with the Joneses, I just want to live better."

Ellis is hampered by cultural habits, too. Like almost all poor evacuees inter-
viewed by *Newsweek*, she has no bank account. Before the storm, she did own a

stereo, refrigerator, washer and dryer, two color TVs and a 1992 Chevy Lumina with more than 100,000 miles on it. This, too, is common among the poor; like more comfortable Americans, they spend on consumer goods beyond their means. But these are often their only assets. The reason that more African-Americans didn't heed warnings to leave New Orleans before the hurricane hit goes beyond the much-publicized lack of cars. They were reluctant to abandon their entire net worth to looters. John Edwards, who has spent much of the year since he lost the vice presidency studying the problems of "the two Americas," says that establishing thousands of bank accounts is critical—not just for Katrina evacuees, but for others in poverty.

Isolation is the second big factor that makes poverty even worse. While racial segregation in housing is at its lowest levels since 1920, Sheryll Cashin, author of "The Failures of Integration," has found that only 5 to 10 percent of American families live in stable, integrated communities. More than half a century after *Brown v. Board of Education*, public schools are still almost totally segregated—the result of where people choose to live, not law. Blacks and whites increasingly go to school with more integrated Hispanics, but not with each other. One big change is that blacks seem only a little more interested in integration than whites.

But there's a steep price to this voluntary segregation. While overt discrimination is dwindling—in part because perpetrators can be successfully sued for practicing it—it still exists. A 1999 University of Pennsylvania study showed that telephone callers using "black English" were offered fewer real-estate choices. At a deeper level, Harvard's Glenn C. Loury has identified what he calls "discrimination in contact." Informal contacts between people across racial lines break down wariness and lead to the connections that help people find jobs. When perfectly legal social segregation prevents blacks from having such informal networks, they slip back.

This isolation has hampered many Katrina evacuees and other inner-city blacks. Joycelyn Harris has spent her whole life in the Ninth Ward. One of 11 children, she dropped out of school at the age of 12 and went on to have five children of her own, later working at Burger King and as a hotel chambermaid. She and her boyfriend, Kenneth Anthony, fled the city last week with nothing but $9 in their pockets and the clothes on their backs. They lived for a time in a New Orleans housing project isolated by two industrial canals and railroad tracks. "Sometimes I wanted to back out, but you can't," says Anthony, who has lived in four different housing projects. "I felt like I was incarcerated."

In the last decade, the government has torn down more than 70,000 units of public housing nationwide, including where Harris and Anthony once lived. But too often, the people who resided there are left to fend for themselves. While everyone agrees that housing vouchers are a good idea, the waiting list to use them for public housing is five years.

Following the Gatreaux model in Chicago, the Clinton administration launched a "scatter-site" housing program in four cities that found homes for the poor in mixed-income neighborhoods. While the move doesn't much benefit adults, their children—confronted with higher expectations and a less harmful peer group—do much better. "It really helped in Atlanta," says Rep. John Lewis, a hero of the civil-rights movement. Bush and the GOP Congress killed the idea, as well as the Youth Opportunity Grant program, which had shown success in partnering with the private sector to help prepare disadvantaged teens for work and life. They tried to cut after-school programs—proven winners—by 40 percent, then settled for a freeze.

The third problem exacerbating poverty is what some call racism. Others argue the word is too inflammatory for a more subtle but no less debilitating effect.

Racism was clearly present in the aftermath of Katrina. Readers of *Yahoo News* noticed it when a pair of waterlogged whites were described in a caption as "carrying" food while another picture (from a different wire service) of blacks holding food described them as "looters." White suburban police closed at least one bridge to keep a group of blacks from fleeing to white areas. Over the course of two days, a white river-taxi operator from hard-hit St. Bernard Parish rescued scores of people from flooded areas and ferried them to safety. All were white. "A n—ger is a n—ger is a n—ger," he told a *Newsweek* reporter. Then he said it again.

Was the slowness of Washington's rescue efforts also a racial thing? In 2004, Bush moved huge resources into Florida immediately following hurricanes there. No one was stranded. The salient difference was not race but politics. Those hurricanes came just before an election.

Obama, the only African-American in the U.S. Senate, says "the ineptitude was colorblind." But he argues that while—contrary to rapper Kanye West's attack on Bush—there was no "active malice," the federal response to Katrina represented "a continuation of passive indifference" on the part of the government. It reflected an unthinking assumption that every American "has the capacity to load up their family in an SUV, fill it up with $100 worth of gasoline, stick some bottled water in the trunk and use a credit card to check into a hotel on safe ground." When they did focus on race in the aftermath, many Louisianans let their fears take over. Lines at gun stores in Baton Rouge, La., snaked out the door. Obama stops short of calling this a sign of racism. For some, he says, it's a product of "sober concern" after the violence in the city; for others, it's closer to "racial stereotyping."

Harvard's Loury argued in a 2002 book, "The Anatomy of Racial Inequality," that it's this stereotyping and "racial stigma," more than overt racism, that helps hold blacks in poverty. Loury explains a destructive cycle of "self-reinforcing stereotypes" at school and work. A white employer, for instance, may make a judgment based on prior experience that the young black men he hires are likely to be absent or late for work. So he supervises them more closely. Resenting the scrutiny, the African-Americans figure that they're being disrespected for no good reason, so they might as well act out, which in turn reinforces their boss's stereotype. Everybody goes away angry.

Such problems are often less about race than class, which has become a huge factor within the black community, too. It's hard for studious young African-Americans to brave the taunts that they're "acting white." The only answer to that is a redoubled effort within the black community to respect academic achievement and a commitment by white institutions to use affirmative action not just for middle-class minorities but for the poor it was originally designed to help.

Beyond the thousands of individual efforts necessary to save New Orleans and ease poverty lie some big political choices. Until Katrina intervened, the top priority for the GOP when Congress reconvened was permanent repeal of the estate tax, which applies to far less than 1 percent of taxpayers. (IRS figures show that only 1,607 wealthy people in Louisiana, Alabama and Mississippi even pay the tax, out of more than 4 million taxpayers—one twenty-fifth of 1 percent.) Repeal would cost the government $24 billion a year. Meanwhile, House GOP leaders are set to slash food stamps by billions in order to protect subsidies to wealthy farmers. But Katrina could change the climate. The aftermath was not a good omen for the Grover Norquists of the world, who want to slash taxes more and shrink government to the size where it can be "strangled in the bathtub."

What kind of president does George W. Bush want to be? He can limit his legacy to Iraq, the war on terror and tax cuts for the rich—or, if he seizes the moment, he could undertake a midcourse correction that might materially change the lives of millions. Katrina gives Bush an only-Nixon-could-go-to-China opportunity, if he wants it.

Margaret Schuber, who evacuated to Atlanta, was a middle-school principal in Jefferson Parish before retiring recently. "I have lived in the city all my life and I didn't realize there were so many people suffering socioeconomically. If you believe in the idea of community, then we all bear responsibility." Schuber is concerned that so many energetic young people aren't planning to return. She's going back to volunteer in the schools. "We all need to do what we can to turn things around," she says.

America was built and saved by the Margaret Schubers of the world. Now we need them again, not just in the midst of an emergency but for the hard work of redemption.

The Changing Face of Poverty in America[*]

By William E. Spriggs

The American Prospect, May 2007

"Water, water everywhere, nor any drop to drink."—Samuel Taylor Coleridge, *The Rime of the Ancient Mariner*

In 1960 American workers produced a gross domestic Product of $13,847 (in year 2000 dollars) for every man, woman, and child in the country. By 1969, GDP per capita rose to $18,578. In that period, the poverty rate for American children dropped almost by half, from 26.5 percent to 13.8 percent. The most recent data, for 2005, show child poverty has risen again, to 17.1 percent, while the GDP per capita stood at $37,246, roughly double the value in 1969. How did the nation become twice as wealthy but its children become poorer?

In 2000, the number of poor Americans reached an 11-year low at 31.6 million, and the poverty rate stood at a 26-year low at 11.3 percent. While the nation again became richer after the post-2001 recovery, more than 5 million Americans fell into poverty, and the latest figures put the number of poor Americans at 36.9 million people.

To put a face on American poverty, it is important to first put that poverty in context—to understand not just who is poor today but to examine how poverty changes over time. With that perspective, we can appreciate that in a nation as wealthy as the United States, poverty is not intractable.

"THE FEDERAL GOVERNMENT DECLARED WAR ON POVERTY, AND POVERTY WON."—RONALD REAGAN

That line from president Reagan's 1988 state of the Union address, was used to ridicule Lyndon Johnson's efforts to fight poverty. President Johnson launched that fight in March 1964, submitting the Economic Opportunity Act to Congress and saying these words: "Because it is right, because it is wise, and because, for the first time in our history, it is possible to conquer poverty . . ."

Johnson believed that a wealthy nation produces enough for each individual citizen to live above poverty. This was a question of political and moral will, not an economic constraint. So, he differentiated between the day's global struggle to end poverty in countries like Mali and Haiti, where there was a real economic constraint to be overcome, and the situation in America, a land that was not poor in resources but that lacked moral conviction. The Johnson legacy chart on the following page shows the path of poverty for black children, a primary beneficiary of LBJ's programs. In 1965, almost 66 percent of black children lived below the poverty line. In four short years, that share was cut to 39.6 percent, a tremendous accomplishment. By contrast, the Reagan legacy chart shows the path of poverty for black children from 1981 to 1989, the era of Reagan and George Bush Senior. In 1980, 42.1 percent of black children lived below the poverty line; and by 1988 that share had risen to 42.8 percent. Yes, poverty won.

HOW POLICY INFLUENCES POVERTY

The face of poverty in America is the result of policy choices, of political will, and of moral conviction—or its absence. The incidence of poverty is heavily concentrated in the United States across the South and the Southwest. The legacy of slavery is part of that story. Forty percent of America's poor live in the South. Four of today's five poorest states were ones that existed in the old Confederacy. Of the onetime Confederate states, only two—Florida and Virginia—do not rank in the current 20 states with highest poverty levels.

Why do some people lack the income to rise above poverty? For many, the reason is that they do not work; for others, the reason is that they work but do not earn enough money. Nonworkers include the elderly, the disabled, and children, as well as the unemployed. And public policy treats different groups differently.

The Social Security old-age program insures virtually all retired workers against the risk of outliving their savings. The old-age benefit formula is tied to the rising productivity of current workers, indexing the benefits to the average national wage. The shared risk, and the insured shared prosperity, explain why the poverty rate for those over 65 has declined from more than 28 percent in 1966 (nearly double the national poverty rate of 14.7 percent) to 10.1 percent today (below the national rate of 12.6 percent). In 1974, the poverty rate for the Census category of white non-Hispanic seniors, at 12.5 percent, was double the poverty rate for working-age (18-64) white non-Hispanics, at 5.9 percent. Today, the poverty rate for the two age groups is virtually equal, at 7.9 percent for seniors and 7.8 percent for working-age white non-Hispanics.

Another group of people who do not work, by law, are children. But their income is derived mostly from their parents. The rise in child poverty, therefore, reflects the rise in the inequality of their parents' earnings. So, while 9.8 percent of the poor are seniors, 33.5 percent of the poor are children. Children make up a much higher share of the poor among blacks (41.9 percent of poor blacks) and Hispanics (42.6 percent of poor Hispanics) than among whites (24.5 percent of poor whites). And while the poverty rate of seniors has shown a steady trend downward as national income has risen, child poverty rates are as intractable as the growing inequality in working families' earnings.

The wide divergence in how public policy treats different groups was not Congress' original intent. The Social Security Act of 1935 sought to protect the incomes of those who did not work because of age or a poor economy by establishing a federal framework for unemployment insurance, old-age benefits, and assistance to women with dependent children. In 1939, the old-age benefit structure was fully federalized to produce consistent benefits. But, Aid to Families with Dependent Children (AFDC) and the unemployment-insurance system were put in state hands. And in the 1990s, AFDC was transformed from its Social Security Act roots into a state block grant. The mostly state-run unemployment-insurance system, meanwhile, is strained by the transformation of the economy from one in which workers could expect to be laid off in recessions and then rehired into one based on the structural creation and destruction of whole industries and occupations.

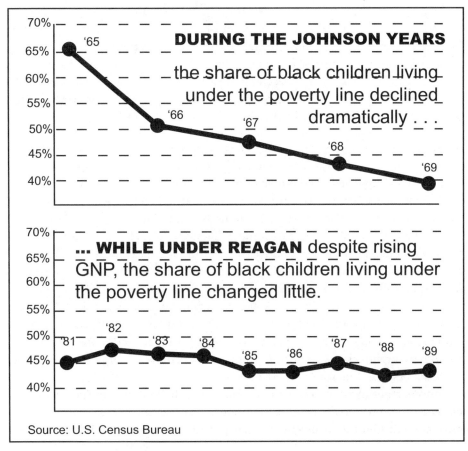

Source: U.S. Census Bureau

Children in our antipoverty system are oddly split. Today, more children receive a check from the Old Age, Survivors, and Disability Insurance (OASDI) Program than are helped by the new Temporary Assistance for Needy Families (TANF) program that replaced AFDC. Some children, therefore, enjoy their parents' protection against the loss of income from disability, untimely death, or old age, and receive benefits that are based on the same formula used for the old-age benefit. Low-income black children are especially helped by the disability benefits their parents receive, or by the survivor benefits that the child receives—because the benefit formula is national and intended to alleviate poverty.

By contrast, children receiving TANF aid are subject to the whim of their state. In 2004, a widowed mother and two children, on average, received a monthly OASDI survivors' benefit of $1,952. Those two children would live above the federal poverty line. The TANF benefit for the same family, however, could range from $170 a month in Mississippi to $215 in Alabama to $240 in Louisiana to $625 in New Hampshire, leaving children in all of those states far below the poverty line. Adjusting for inflation, the survivors' benefit has been increasing since 1970, while the average benefit under AFDC (and now TANF) has been falling. While the OASDI benefit level is set by a federal formula, policy-makers in states with higher shares of black TANF recipients choose lower benefit levels.

Like TANF recipients, unemployed workers are also at the mercy of their state; the average weekly benefit can range from $179 a week in Mississippi to $320 in New Jersey. In the 1950s, close to half of the nation's unemployed workers received benefits; today, only about 35 percent do. This varies widely by state, from 21 percent in Wyoming to 24 percent in Texas to 58 percent in Pennsylvania to 71 percent in New Jersey. And the percentage of earned income replaced by unemployment benefits has steadily fallen as well.

DILIGENT AND STILL POOR

An ongoing topic of debate is the relationship of child poverty and parents' income to the increase in single-parent households. Other things being equal, two parents in a household usually earn more than one, but they are not assured of earning their family's way out of poverty. Hispanic and black children have roughly similar levels of poverty—33.2 percent for black children, and 27.7 percent for Hispanic children. Yet 41 percent of black families with children are married, whereas 68 percent of Hispanic families with children are married. In 1974, when the poverty rate among black children was at 39.6 percent, 56 percent of black families with children were married. Two-income families today are less likely to be poor, but much is at work besides family structure.

To be poor is to lack income, so the core issue is earnings. In 1962, on the eve of the March on Washington for Jobs and Justice in 1963, the median income of black men was below the poverty threshold for a family of three, but by 1967 it was above that level (not until 1995 did it get above the poverty level for a family of four). Because of the rise in the earnings of black women, poverty among black children fell in the 1990s, just as the rise in the earnings of black men helped lower black children's poverty level in the 1960s. By 1997, the median income of black women rose above the poverty level for a family of three.

Among the poor, 11.4 percent work full time, year-round. These 2.9 million Americans are directly hurt by minimum-wage laws that have lagged behind costs of living. This problem is especially acute for Asians and Hispanics, where 18 percent of the working poor worked full time, year-round.

Recent immigrants who are not citizens have a poverty rate of 20.4 percent. Like all groups, noncitizen immigrants had falling poverty rates in the 1990s as the labor market expanded: Their poverty rate fell from 28.7 percent in 1993 to a low of 19.2 percent in 2000. Then, following the national trend, their poverty rate started to climb. During the Reagan administration, the United States suffered its highest national unemployment rates since the Great Depression. In the black community, the effects were devastating: The unemployment rate for adult (over age 20) black men peaked at more than 20 percent in December 1982; during the entire Reagan presidency, the unemployment rate for adult black men remained in double digits. The highest recorded unemployment rate for adult white men was 9 percent in November and December 1982. But for black men, the unemployment rate remained above that mark for 182 straight months (15 years), from October 1979 to November 1994. Because children do not work and need working adults to support them, it is hardly surprising that during that period, black child poverty rates remained intractable above 40 percent.

Poverty for women is disproportionately higher than for men, 14.1 percent compared to 11.1 (in 2005), primarily because of higher rates of poverty among female-headed households, gaps in poverty for the elderly (7.3 percent for men over age 65 compared to 12.3 percent for women in 2005), and for single women (24.1 percent) compared to single men (17.9 percent) living alone. The gap reflects

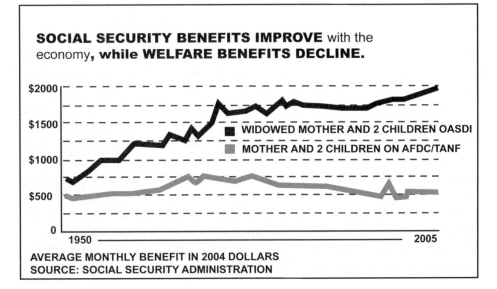

SOCIAL SECURITY BENEFITS IMPROVE with the economy**, while WELFARE BENEFITS DECLINE.**

- ■ WIDOWED MOTHER AND 2 CHILDREN OASDI
- ■ MOTHER AND 2 CHILDREN ON AFDC/TANF

$2000 / $1500 / $1000 / $500 / 0

1950 — 2005

AVERAGE MONTHLY BENEFIT IN 2004 DOLLARS
SOURCE: SOCIAL SECURITY ADMINISTRATION

persistent gaps in earnings between men and women, though that gap is falling. White non-Hispanic men, age 25 and over, with a high-school diploma have a median income of $35,679, while women, age 25 and over, need a college degree to have a similar median income ($36,532 in 2005). And, while the median income of white males has been above the poverty line for a family of five since 1959, the median income for women only broke above the poverty line for a family of three in 1990. The persistent gap is best reflected in differences in poverty among the elderly, where the life-long earnings of women mean they have lower assets in Social Security benefits than do men, despite the progressive structure of the benefit formula. The gap among the elderly also reflects issues of access to jobs with pensions for women.

Women who are the single head of household face the extra burden of earning enough to raise dependent children out of poverty. This risk a woman faces of helping non-working dependents is not shared by society, as would be a woman's efforts to care for her elderly parents. The result is that female-headed households, harmed by the significant earnings gap between men and women, have a poverty rate of 31.1 percent compared to male-headed households (with no wife present) of 13.4 percent, while the overall poverty rate for families is 10.8 percent.

FULL EMPLOYMENT AND ITS LIMITS

It took the presidency of Bill Clinton, with its expansive labor market and increases in the minimum wage and the Earned Income Tax Credit, to dramatically improve the incomes of poor and minority families. As job creation reached a record pace, the unemployment rate for black men plummeted, reaching a recorded low of 6 percent in March 1999. With work comes income, and poverty for black families fell. This history suggests something about the proper way to view responsibility and poor people as agents in their own fate: Usually they are not victims of themselves, but of bad economic policies and barriers to opportunity.

Under Reagan, who ridiculed antipoverty efforts, the number of black children living below the poverty line increased by 200,000, from 3.9 million in 1980 to 4.1 million in 1988. During the Clinton years, the black child poverty rate fell steadily, from 46.3 percent to a record-low 30 percent, lifting about 1.6 million black children out of poverty. For all children, the poverty rate fell annually during Clinton's presidency, reaching a 30-year low of 15.6 percent when he left office. But those reduced poverty rates may be the best we can achieve simply by getting jobs for parents. While lower than during the Reagan years, they do not equal the lows America has achieved for its senior citizens, or the general population. And those gains reversed course when George W. Bush became president.

Because of record job creation in the 1990s, the number of people who worked and were poor declined from 10.1 million in 1993 to 8.5 million by 2000; greatly increased working hours and higher wages meant higher incomes. But during the current expansion, a record 48 months was required to get payroll employment back to the level preceding the employment downturn that began in late 2000, a lag not matched since Herbert Hoover. So while full employment is necessary to alleviate poverty, it is far from sufficient.

In short, America knows how to address poverty. Its great success in lowering the poverty level of those over 65 has changed the face of poverty. But for those subject to the whims of state differences and the correlation of race with state policies to address poverty, there have been great intractable issues that have left the face of poverty disproportionately young, black, Hispanic, and female. Growing inequality in the labor market, moreover, has increased the share of the poor who are of working age, and stagnant federal minimum-wage laws have increased the oxymoron of full-time, year-round working poor people.

In a nation with a per capita GDP above the poverty line for a family of four, it is appalling that almost 3 million people work full time, year-round and are poor, and that more than 12 million American children are living in poverty. Lyndon Johnson proposed to fight poverty "because it is right, because it is wise." In a land of vast wealth, twice as rich as America in the 1960s, can today's leaders rise to the occasion?

Poverty Row[*]

By Jeffrey M. Jones
Hoover Digest, Summer 2007

The biblical phrase "the poor you always have with you" seems to have particular resonance for presidential campaigns. Every four years poverty regains its prominence as voters ponder the candidates' views on a spectrum of values-based issues. Where do this year's would-be presidents stand on helping America's poor and what would they do if elected? And does either of the two warring parties feature any standout candidates on the problem of poverty?

Thanks to the Pew Forum on Religion and Public Life, voters can get a head start on probing the most pressing issues of campaign '08, poverty included. The website, Religion and Politics '08 (http://pewforum.org/religion08) offers profiles of the major candidates using a number of lenses: abortion, church and state, the death penalty, education, the environment, faith-based initiatives, gay marriage, health care, immigration, the Iraq war, poverty, and stem cell research.

By mid-spring, the Pew Forum had posted poverty profiles on eight candidates—Sam Brownback, Rudy Giuliani, John McCain, and Mitt Romney on the Republican side; Hillary Clinton, John Edwards, Barack Obama, and Bill Richardson among the Democrats.

One striking feature is the common ground among left and right. None of the major candidates views welfare reform as a failure. Indeed, the front-runners on each side—Clinton and Giuliani—have consistently advocated improving the lives of poor Americans through work. As the then mayor of New York, Giuliani famously implemented the reform efforts signed into law by Clinton's husband. One would be hard-pressed today to find anyone in the mainstream arguing for "welfare rights" or a return to the entitlement mentality that was done away with in 1996 after more than 60 years of failing to end poverty.

Another area of agreement is support for increasing the minimum wage. Of the eight candidates profiled, only one, Kansas senator Brownback, appears to oppose minimum-wage increases without reservation. The other Republicans (Giuliani,

McCain, and Romney) have shown a willingness to raise it under certain conditions, a position generally opposed in conservative circles. This more moderate position has opened up the three to charges of flip-flopping for political ends. The four Democrats, however, risk nothing by fully backing minimum-wage increases during the primaries. The Left grows louder and bolder each and every year that the federal minimum wage remains at $5.15 an hour; regulating private wages, says the Left, is good for workers, good for employers, and good for the economy. Ronald Reagan ('Outside of its legitimate function, government does nothing as well or as economically as the private sector') might beg to differ.

Subtle differences appear in the tone and rhetoric used to describe the candidates' views. Whether the Pew Forum is taking its cues from the speeches or employing selective quotations, the Democrats (Richardson excepted) sound as though they care for the poor, whereas the Republicans seem concerned only about policy. Whether it's Clinton's promise that the middle class "will no longer be ignored," Obama's call for a "stronger sense of empathy," or Edwards's declaration that poverty is "the great moral issue of our time," the blue party is all heart. But it was Brownback who spent two nights in a prison reaching out to "the poor and dispossessed," Giuliani who became a Republican only after realizing that compassion means sharing with the poor "the solutions that work for everybody," and Romney who finally brought true welfare reform to Massachusetts, nine years after passage of the federal law, "to give welfare recipients the opportunity to achieve independent and fulfilling lives."

Another facet of the candidates' antipoverty stances appears in a Pew Forum profile on health care, where the partisan divide is much clearer. Although there is some agreement on the problem—too many low-income, uninsured families—health care otherwise offers a classic dividing line between Republicans and Democrats. Every Republican candidate supports reform efforts based on free-market principles; increased competition, targeted regulation, subsidies that help the poor buy private insurance, and greater freedom of choice are seen as the best ways to improve our healthcare system without impairing the level of care. All the Democrats, by contrast, favor a different flavor of universal health care and are generally not content with mandating universal coverage on a private insurance system. Indeed, Obama, Edwards, and Clinton would probably pursue some form of government-run health insurance for all Americans.

OF ONE HEART

Too many voters stop examining politicians and positions when they reach the end of their preferred voter guides. But digging into the details is the only way to gain an informed perspective on a candidate's qualifications and his or her justifications for the policies proposed. Two candidates, former senator John Edwards of North Carolina and Senator Sam Brownback of Kansas, most strongly articulate a passion for the poor.

Edwards, in a major policy address in June 2006, stated, "How we respond to the fact that millions among us live in poverty says everything about the character of America." Brownback's compassionate agenda is motivated by his concern for "the poor, the downtrodden, those without a voice, those in difficult circumstances," according to an article in the *Weekly Standard*.

Although both were trailing the front-runners in their respective parties by double-digit margins in mid-spring, they are experienced political operatives who cannot be overlooked. Brownback won a second term in the Senate in 2004 by a landslide, not losing a single county in his state. That same year, the Kerry-Edwards ticket fell one state shy (approximately 60,000 votes) of securing the White House.

In addition to political savvy, the two candidates have had similar experiences in coming to their views on the issue of poverty. Each credits a spiritual shake-up in the mid-1990s with refocusing him on a poverty agenda. Brownback, who was diagnosed with skin cancer in 1995, said his illness led to "a lot of internal examination." He credits his love for God with animating his love for others and says that explains "my focus on Africa, the poor, on racial reconciliation." Edwards, in similar fashion, saw his "faith come roaring back" in response to the tragic death of his 16-year-old son in 1996. The former senator's revitalized faith "informs everything I think and do. It's part of my value system," he said in an interview. Those values include Edwards's focus on poverty, health care, and humanitarian issues in Africa.

The common interest in international aid is significant; both candidates have traveled overseas to combat poverty in the earth's most desperate regions. Brownback, in particular, is noted on both sides of the aisle for his co-sponsorship of the Trafficking Victims Protection Act. In addition, the two senators share a fondness for the motif of "second chances." Edwards has proposed funding "second-chance schools" that give dropouts the opportunity to earn a diploma and the potentially higher wages that go with it. Brownback has put forth a Second Chance Act aimed at reducing the recidivism of newly released prisoners through "housing, drug treatment, counseling, job training, and education."

OF TWO MINDS

But a common passion for fighting poverty does not translate into a shared understanding of what constitutes effective change. There exists, in Thomas Sowell's words, "a conflict of visions" between Brownback and Edwards.

Edwards's solutions are articulated in several themes carried over from the previous presidential campaign, when he was John Kerry's running mate: first, that there is merit in emphasizing the distinctions between the haves and the have-nots, or what he refers to as the "Two Americas," and that pointing out the disparity will motivate change. Edwards is convinced that Hurricane Katrina was a stark demonstration of the Two Americas, with the private response showing that we "want to live in one America." But Katrina was an equal-opportunity destroyer, and the overwhelming personal charity that continues to this day points to a nation already capable of uniting to help even its poorest people.

Edwards's second theme is that government is uniquely suited to develop incentives to encourage the right kinds of behavior. To get the poor to work, Edwards proposes what he calls a "Working Society," using government-sponsored health benefits, tax cuts, wage increases, tax credits, savings bonds, and housing vouchers to convince people that it pays to work, as though work itself could never be a reward. Edwards says, "In return for greater investments, we would expect everyone who can work to work, for the sake of their country, their families, and themselves." And thanks to the federal government for making it happen.

Edwards's final theme is cast as a bold vision—a national goal of eliminating poverty in the next 30 years. But it should truly be dubbed a multi-billion-dollar pipe dream. His vision could cost $15 billion to $20 billion as it establishes a massive new federal effort to "create a million more housing vouchers . . . and one million 'stepping-stone' jobs over five years." Edwards's plan for ending poverty makes one wonder where the greatest poverty-fighting, wealth-producing mechanism in the history of world—the U.S. economy—fits into his agenda.

Brownback's approach differs markedly, filtering poverty solutions through a series of tests to ensure that they will be in the United States' best interests, free of the effects that produce dependency and favorable to the interests of the family. Fighting poverty overseas, especially in Africa, is about defending the dignity of people "no matter where they are, no matter what they look like, no matter what their status." But it also serves the U.S. national interest in promoting democracy, fighting the spread of disease, checking China's natural-resource grabs, and eliminating safe havens for terrorists.

In contrast to Edwards's government-led approach, Brownback is wary of repeating mistakes, especially the kind that led to welfare dependency over many generations. Several of his legislative and policy positions seek to counter such dependency in its various forms. Thus he is a strong supporter of faith-based programs because they have "measurable results," often exceeding those of similar government programs. His support for prisoner re-entry programs helps overcome a perverse cycle of dependency, "breaking the generational curse . . . so that it doesn't go to your kids and grandkids. Even the senator's efforts to combat human trafficking can be seen as casting aside archaic and inhumane dependency relationships.

The final way in which Brownback hopes to fight poverty is his desire to "rebuild the culture and the family." Government is often to blame when American culture fails to support the family; for example, welfare laws penalize the poor for getting married (one can lose up to 88 percent of his or her benefits), even though marriage is one of the most statistically significant factors for escaping poverty. Brownback has highlighted a two-year-old federal pilot program that features "marriage development accounts" that support low-income couples through educational, financial, and life-skills training. It also matches personal savings at a rate of $3 to $1. In Brownback's estimation, as the family goes, so goes the culture. Thus, antipoverty efforts that affirm strong families are the key not just to each individual's welfare but to the welfare of the nation.

A spring 2007 Harris Poll listed programs for the poor as just inside the top 25 most important issues for government to address—well behind the war in Iraq, the economy, and education. But several other key issues, including health care, immigration, and jobs, directly bear on reducing poverty in America. The plight of the poor still troubles us as a nation, motivates us to action as individuals, and matters to us in the leaders we choose. Here's hoping we choose wisely.

Poverty Is Back!*

By Ezra Klein
American Prospect, January 16, 2006

It was 1988, Ronald Reagan's final State of the Union. The previous eight years had been good to the Gipper. The word "iberal" had been rendered radioactive, many items on the conservative wish list had been checked off, and Reagan himself had stomped two successive Democratic challengers. So you might think he would have been content to ride quietly into the sunset, a conservative legend retiring athwart a horse named History. But that night, Reagan stuck a final knife in the battered, bloodied carcass of liberalism. As was his wont, he did it with a grin: "My friends," he said. "Some years ago, the federal government declared war on poverty, and poverty won. [Laughter.] Today, the federal government has 59 major welfare programs and spends more than $100 billion a year on them. What has all this money done?"

The jab was classic Reagan. Even now, the chuckles echo, preserved in the transcript as stage direction for future conservatives. But, in classically Reaganesque fashion, the line lacked a sort of historical, well, accuracy. The money had done much. The Great Society had not failed, its programs were not bureaucratic black holes whirling destructively through the inner city. While poverty had indeed weathered Lyndon Johnson's assault, it stumbled forth a withered shell of its former self. Where in 1959 it could claim a robust membership of 22.4 percent of Americans, by 1973 it was at an emaciated 11.1 percent. In 2004, it rested at 12.7 percent.

And there's good reason for that success. Since Lyndon Johnson, only the two Presidents Bush failed to substantively address poverty. Richard Nixon created Supplemental Security Income and considered guaranteeing a minimum yearly wage, Gerald Ford resurrected the Earned Income Tax Credit (EITC), Jimmy Carter passed the Comprehensive Employment and Training Administration Act, and even Ronald Reagan vastly expanded the EITC. To paraphrase Bush's favorite philosopher, the poor we have always had with us, even during Republican administrations.

But for conservatives, halting attempts to eradicate poverty slowly gave way to more successful efforts to vilify it. Conservative leaders kept a dark (literally and figuratively) picture of the underclass visible to the nation's white middle class. The faces of poverty became more sinister: the Willie Hortons and the Linda Taylors (Linda Taylor was Reagan's ubiquitous welfare queen whose ill-gotten payouts totaled no more than $8,000). These visages transformed a discussion over alleviating economic despair into a subtly racist wedge issue that resonated with white males. And so it was easier, after that, to suggest that, irrespective of the facts, the Great Society was a disaster, poverty the intractable affliction of an unsocialized underclass. Egghead liberals with more good intentions than common sense had surrendered to instinct and offered cash prizes to every unwed black mother able to bear a child, creating a culture of government dependency that fostered criminality, broken families, and joblessness.

Conservatives, deciding government involvement had created the problem, concluded that government withdrawal would solve it. But Clinton's ascension and Democratic sympathy for the poor wrecked that plan, and the two sides eventually compromised on a sort of political detente they termed welfare reform. Welfare reform, while about poor people, was never about poverty, it was about politics. It made the impoverished a little less galling to the better off, ensuring that the government's incentive structure didn't reward the out-of-work and thus offend the gainfully employed. Meanwhile, crime was plummeting and the streets, thanks to Bill Clinton's 1994 Crime Bill, were flooded with new police officers. Come the late 1990s, the poor were neither dangerous nor ideologically maddening. A handful of urban politicians continued pleading for inner-city aid, but with electoral power shifting away from metropolitan centers, few listened. After 9-11, no one did. Poor blacks were no longer the threat; poor browns had taken their place. And so America's impoverished became something new: forgotten.

And then the waters came. Katrina's images washed away the country's comfortable "see-no, hear-no, speak-no evil" approach to poverty. The middle class rediscovered the underclass, and that meant the political class had to address the excavation. George W. Bush even located his inner Lyndon Johnson for the occasion. Seventeen days after Katrina slammed into Louisiana, Bush said: "As all of us saw on television, there is also some deep, persistent poverty in this region as well. And that poverty has roots in a history of racial discrimination, which cut off generations from the opportunity of America. We have a duty to confront this poverty with bold action. So let us restore all that we have cherished from yesterday, and let us rise above the legacy of inequality."

It might have been a moment for progressives to step forth. After all, Katrina offered an instant of true moral outrage at economic inequality, and no one thought Bush was serious about tackling racism or poverty himself. The trouble was, progressives were not ready to respond. The important question is why.

The obvious, and easiest, answer is that they lacked the power. But while electoral defeats help explain why Democrats couldn't implement a comprehensive antipoverty strategy, they don't account for why they couldn't propose one. It's not just that Democrats couldn't bring policies onto the Senate floor. In this case, the backstage was empty too. The Democratic National Committee's issues page never mentions the word "poverty." Nor does Harry Reid's, Nancy Pelosi's, the House Democratic Caucus, nor the Senate Democratic Caucus. Not a single one identifies poverty as an issue the Democratic Party cares to solve. That's largely because, politically, poverty hasn't proven a winning issue for Democrats over the past couple of decades. Reagan and Gingrich brandished it as a weapon and Clinton's welfare reform almost tore the Democratic Party apart. So it's little wonder that when the moment came to address it, the party was caught unprepared.

Nonetheless, the policy weapons available to combat poverty have multiplied. They've become smarter, subtler, and electorally safer. Think tanks and academic journals hum with innovative, politically savvy approaches to poverty that reward work and thrift, encourage education and ownership, and protect against fate's nastier whims. These proposals have adeptly structured their incentives to fulfill the unfinished promise of welfare reform: Do right and you'll do well. Where the 1996 bill succeeded primarily in cleansing the welfare rolls, these approaches make manifest the welfare reform consensus that work should serve as the path out of poverty. So far there has not been the political will forcing these solutions into the public debate. But that can change.

So where to begin? First, by understanding that, contrary to popular belief, there's no straight line connecting the economic sins of the father to the impoverishment of the son. Seventy percent of those in poverty ascend out of it within three years, while only 12 percent remain for more than a decade. Unfortunately, it is also recurrent, with about half of those who escape dipping back beneath the poverty line within four years. Indeed, poverty is a primarily transitory condition anchored by a perpetually poor minority.

All of which is to say that there are different types of poverty, many causes, and countless avenues of approach. But a few overarching problems stick out: Almost half of all bankruptcies have a major, if not sole, medical component, and even quick spells of being uninsured at unlucky times can lead to bills stretching far beyond $10,000 and create massive debt. Debt becomes a second major problem for the poor, who, lacking fallback savings, are particularly vulnerable to predatory lenders. Third, at base, the ebbs and flows of poverty tell a story of proportionally unequal income growth. The minimum wage is at a 56-year low compared to the average hourly wage, a depreciation that is also diminishing the worth of the earned income tax credit, and thus battering the total take-home pay of low-income workers.

But these problems, while tricky, are not intractable. What follows is a rough synthesis of progressive policy solutions to poverty, though not the only ones possible. Housing, unions, education all deserve more attention. In addition, there are endless permutations, variations, and alternatives to the proposals laid out here, but these offer, if nothing else, a starting point and model for that discussion.

ASSET-BUILDING

Assets are economic air bags. When a financial crunch comes, they inflate, softening the blow. Periods of unemployment can be endured while the wage earner searches for high-quality positions, lessening the chance he'll accept a lower-paying or less secure job. And assets work to lift families out of poverty as well. They're what send a child to private school or college, purchase a car so a parent can take a better job farther away, or provide the down payment on a home. Without them, these affirmative steps often can't happen and, if they do, they carry the threat and even promise of crushing, lasting debt.

Assets also offer the starkest illustration of the country's economic inequities. When the measure is a family's yearly pay, whites take home $55,768, blacks net $34,369, and Hispanics make $34,262. Roughly divided, blacks and Hispanics make 61 percent of what whites make. Wealth, however, is another story: White households have an average $88,651 in assets. Hispanics have $7,932 and blacks $5,988. A quick trip back to the calculator shows that Hispanics have nine percent as much wealth as whites, while blacks command a bit less than seven percent.

The most politically attractive form of asset building focuses on the most sympathetic of entitlement targets: children. In 2005, the UK passed Child Trust Funds (CTFs) into law. CTFs are tax-free bank accounts given to all children and seeded with 250 pounds (a bit less than $450), more if the family is poorer, and yet more when the child turns seven. Families can then put up to 1,200 pounds a year into the tax-protected account, which can only be accessed by the child and only when he or she turns 18.

In the United States, the America Saving for Personal Investment, Retirement, and Education (ASPIRE) Act is a similar piece of legislation with a fair amount of support. But some progressives want to take it even further. One way would be Children's Retirement Accounts. Every year until age six, the government would deposit $1,000 dollars into a tax-free account. At 18, the money could be borrowed at advantageous rates for certain pre-approved purposes (down payment on a home, college tuition, etc.); otherwise, it would continue to collect interest and form the start of retirement savings.

Similar proposals range from work bonds that would give low-income families participating in the workforce for five years $5,000 toward a first home, to Individual Homestead Accounts that would incentivize various life "goalposts" via deposits into a savings account. The best of these plans also allow for emergency borrowing at low rates for certain purposes (transportation breakdowns, etc.), thus allowing the poor to avoid the predatory lending market that "serves" them.

In design, at least, all the asset programs achieve an essentially similar outcome: the creation of wealth that can be used to forge ahead in life. Since their uses are mostly restricted to investment, they aren't very good airbags, but they're power-ful accelerators. That's fine, because the next step is for progressives to protect all Americans from health disasters, ensuring that the most effective sort of airbags come standard with birth.

HEALTH

You know the statistics. Over 45 million Americans are uninsured. Another 16 million are in the nebulous "underinsured" category. Add into the mix the fact that poor health strongly correlates with low incomes, and the massive, economi-cally destabilizing influence of America's patchwork, private health-care system crystallizes.

Right now, health costs are bankrupting big businesses, crushing small business-es, destabilizing the middle class, and generally wreaking economic havoc across society. These problems, again, are most likely to hit the poor who—unlikely to work for employers with affordable and comprehensive health plans—are hurled into the individual market, where insurance companies coldly recoup discounts offered to larger, richer, healthier pools by fleecing those lacking the numbers to bargain. Many others are simply priced out of health care altogether, particularly those unlucky enough to suffer from a preexisting condition. Inevitably, medical emergencies strike, the poor are rushed in for care, and they stagger out in debt.

On one level, the poor have Medicaid. Kind of. Medicaid, originally created to cover those unable to work, relies on a complex and anachronistic system of "cat-egorical" eligibility that relies on certain shifting combinations of being old, ill, pregnant, a parent, and poor. Worse, the system is a federal-state partnership, no two states have the same eligibility rules, and many attempt to further complicate and toughen their standards in order to dissuade new and costly enrollees. So not only are many low-income folks ineligible, among those who are eligible, many don't know how to or can't follow up to enroll.

One option would be to simply fix Medicaid, junking categorical eligibility, tying eligibility to certain percentages of the poverty line, and instituting a shifting scale that allows for low-cost buy-in as incomes rise. Lynn Etheredge and Judith Moore proposed just such a reform in 2003 in Health Affairs. But as each successive year of budget cuts shows, Medicaid is a deeply vulnerable program, particularly in pe-riods of conservative control. That's partly structural: With no dedicated revenue stream and a state-federal funding scheme, the instinct is for both Congress and states to slash the program and blame the other. In addition, little is easier than displaying budgetary restraint by bravely cutting health subsidies for the poor.

The answer to this vulnerability, as we've known since FDR, is universalizing programs so the middle class has a stake in their survival. The sharply different political fortunes of Medicaid and Medicare show that clearly. Most developed nations have government-run systems that provide better care at lower cost, but after Clinton's 1994 health-care reform debacle, there's little appetite for a second run at any quasi-statist reconstruction. Nevertheless, there is a sort of consensus emerging in progressive circles that the Federal Employee Health Benefits Program (FEHBP) offers an attractive avenue for reform.

Widely admired (even on the right) for its efficiency and degree of choice, FEHBP is a collection of federally regulated private insurers who cover more than eight million federal employees. FEHBP could be opened to all Americans and businesses, with low-income individuals enjoying full or partial subsidization based on their relation to the poverty line. Health insurance, much like car insurance, would be made mandatory, and a variety of regulatory changes could refocus private insurers on quality and bringing technological and structural coherence to the system (likely modeled on the wildly successful Veterans Administration network). Widespread adoption of information technology could save more than $80 billion, while a large enough pool would allow cost restraints to control premiums.

This approach rationalizes and guarantees health coverage for the poor, while ensuring the program's strength and sustainability by investing the middle class, and even portions of the business class, in the progressive reform agenda. The Great Society may not have been a policy failure, but it eventually became a political albatross, partially (though not solely) due to the demographic specificity of its programs. There's no reason health coverage should be constructed with the same weakness.

MAKING WORK PAY (ENOUGH)

Of course, not every policy can be universal in its payouts, but every policy can be universal in its moral appeal. The lesson of welfare reform was not that Americans were cheap, but that they were work-oriented. Welfare reform cost more than mere welfare did, but the addition of work requirements was judged worth the expense. Voters decided that those unwilling to work were undeserving of subsidization, but agreed that all who sought and kept employment should find economic dignity within reach.

But work, increasingly, does not pay, or at least not enough. Wage growth has slowed radically, lagging far behind the increases in productivity of the past few years. During late 2004, inflation accelerated past wages, meaning salaries lost ground compared to costs. But even that understates the ever-disintegrating position of low-wage workers. While wage growth across the economy has been slight, there's been growth nonetheless. For the bottom ten percent of wage earners, however, salaries actually fell by ten percent between 1979 and 1999, while the proportion earning wages below the poverty line jumped from 23.7 percent to 26.8 percent.

Good wages, of course, are the key to a stable economic lifestyle. Progressives talk a lot about housing policy, but as Bruce Katz, formerly Henry Cisnero's chief of staff at the Department of Housing and Urban Development, told me, "the housing problems in this country are principally about the gap between wages and prices. . . . We think of housing policy in very narrow, boxed terms. We need to redefine it to include income policy." That goes, basically, for everything. Food stamps are great, but unnecessary on an adequate salary. Few progressives will utter an unkind word about heating subsidies, but those would be similarly redundant if the working class routinely made enough to cover electricity costs in the first place. So, despite the need for programs targeting specific material deprivations, the broader solution is better wage supports.

The first step, then, is a serious increase in the minimum wage. This is key, and not just for the stereotypical pimpled teenagers passing time before graduation: Only one in five minimum-wage workers is younger than 20 and the average minimum-wage worker uses that salary to provide a full 68 percent of his family's total income. Sure, *The Wall Street Journal* will cry buckets over such a blow to our delicate economy, but Clinton's 1996 minimum-wage boost from $4.25 to the current $5.15, which lifted pay for over 9.9 million workers, defied conservative warnings of widespread job decimation. Between 1996 and 2000, unemployment dropped from 5.6 percent to 4 percent. Of the current proposals drifting around Congress, the most likely advocates a three-year phase-in to a minimum wage of $7.50. According to the Economic Policy Institute, hiking the minimum wage to $7.25 would impact 7.7 million workers, 2.2 million fewer than Clinton did, making increased economic distortion highly unlikely.

But a one-time hike, while beneficial, will, due to inflation, rapidly decline in utility. For that reason, progressives should agitate for legislation making minimum wage increases automatic, though with provisions allowing congressional intervention during special economic circumstances. Common proposals here focus on inflation, which makes sense, but has proven politically difficult. More attractive may be tying the minimum wage to productivity, which has grown steadily (and, in recent years, rapidly) and seems a politically intuitive place to peg the wage—if workers are producing more, why shouldn't they be making more?

Raising the minimum wage would also help the Earned Income Tax Credit. The EITC is a tax-based wage subsidy for low-income workers that kicks in at varying strengths depending on family composition and salary level. By subsidizing low-wage work (in some cases, significantly so), it encourages employment, and has emerged as the most successful antipoverty program in the country. Because of the way the EITC is calculated, the declining minimum wage has sparked a decline in the value of most families' EITC. Lifting the minimum wage would strengthen it. The EITC's only problems, really, are mind-bogglingly complex eligibility formulas that contain a marriage penalty. Simplify the eligibility system, eliminate the marriage penalty, and increase the funding to ensure a decent wage. Work shouldn't just pay, it should pay enough.

Progressives backing these proposals should not fear they'll be stepping out of the political mainstream. Americans cherish the concept that all who work can succeed, which is why ballot initiatives to raise the minimum wage routinely return results in the high 70s and why the EITC was signed by Gerald Ford and expanded by Ronald Reagan. Similarly, on health care, nearly 80 percent agree that they'd accept higher taxes to ensure that all have easy access to a doctor. And asset programs are beginning to pick up wide and varied supporters, with everyone from Rick Santorum to Harold Ford jumping atop the ASPIRE bandwagon. Indeed, what's so alluring about these proposals is their political practicability. That Democrats haven't spent more time agitating for their comprehensive implementation is testament to how deeply welfare reform scarred the party.

Thankfully, some Democrats are taking up the conversation again, most notably John Edwards, who is constructing a political platform almost exclusively devoted to combating poverty and inequality. He's also engaged in the project— slightly scary for Democrats—of rearticulating the moral imperative of poverty eradication. When we spoke in early December, his policies were still in a formative stage but his passion for the impoverished Americans that Democrats have spent ten years avoiding was fully developed. "I've sat with these people and they don't think anyone is speaking for them. They don't even have a notion of what having a champion would be like. . . . We can galvanize this country around important issues like this."

Poverty will not vanish on its own. Last time it faced down government, it was slashed in half. But the Vietnam War and the country's swing right simultaneously allowed it to escape and ensured that there'd be no quick pursuit. Forty years later, it's time for round two. And that means progressives had better start training.

We Don't Need Another War on Poverty[*]

As the Urbanism of the Nineties Showed, Cities Can Forge Their Own Futures

By Stephen Malanga
City Journal, Autumn 2008

Do our cities need another War on Poverty? Barack Obama thinks so. Speaking before the U.S. Conference of Mayors this June, the Democratic standard-bearer promised to boost spending on public schools, urban infrastructure, affordable housing, crime prevention, job training, and community organizing. The mayors, joined by many newspaper editorial pages, have echoed Obama in calling for vast new federal spending on cities. All of this has helped rejuvenate the old argument that America's urban areas are victims of Washington's neglect and that it's up to the rest of the country (even though most Americans are now metro-dwellers) to bail them out.

Nothing could be more misguided than to renew this "tin-cup urbanism," as some have called it. Starting in the late 1960s, mayors in struggling cities extended their palms for hundreds of billions of federal dollars that accomplished little good and often worsened the problems that they sought to fix. Beginning in the early nineties, however, a small group of reform-minded mayors—with New York's Rudy Giuliani and Milwaukee's John Norquist in the vanguard—jettisoned tin-cup urbanism and began developing their own bottom-up solutions to city problems. Their innovations made cities safer, put welfare recipients to work, and offered kids in failing school systems new choices, bringing about an incomplete, but very real, urban revival.

Yet this reform movement remains anathema to many liberal politicians, academics, and journalists, who have ignored or tried to downplay its achievements because it conflicts with their left-of-center views. The arrival on the scene of Obama, a former Chicago community activist and the first presidential nominee in recent memory to rise out of urban politics, has given these back-to-the-future voices their best chance in years to advance a liberal War on Poverty–style agenda. As the nation debates its future in the current presidential race, it's crucial to remember what has worked to revive cities—and what hasn't.

The original War on Poverty, launched by the Johnson administration in the mid-sixties, was based on the assumption that Washington had to rescue American cities from precipitous—indeed, catastrophic—decline. It's important to remember that the cities themselves helped propel that decline. Political machines had long run the cities, and they imposed increasingly high taxes and throttling regulations on employers and often entrusted key government agencies, including police departments, to patronage appointees. The cities' industrial might protected them from serious downturns for a time. But as transportation advances beginning in the 1950s enabled businesses to relocate to less expensive suburbs or newer Sunbelt cities, and did so just as a generation of poor, uneducated blacks from the rural South began migrating to the urban North, the corrupt and inefficient machines proved unable to cope with the resulting economic and demographic shock. Urban poverty worsened (even as poverty was shrinking dramatically elsewhere); crime exploded; public schools, dominated by reform-resistant, inflexible teachers' unions, became incubators of failure, with staggering dropout rates for minority students; and middle-class city dwellers soon followed businesses out of town. Some industrial cities, scarred further by horrific race riots during the sixties, crumbled into near-ruins.

Yet the War on Poverty's legislative architects ignored the cities' own failings and instead embraced the theories of left-wing intellectuals, who argued that the external forces arrayed against the poor, such as racism or globalization, were simply too overwhelming to address on the local level. "Officials and residents in urban communities are losing control of their cities to outside forces," warned urban planners Edward Kaitz and Herbert Harvey Hyman in their book *Urban Planning for Social Welfare.* "Cities are relatively powerless." The answer was federal intervention. Columbia University's Frances Fox Piven and Richard Cloward gained an influential following among policymakers by arguing that an unjust and racist nation owed massive government aid to the poor and mostly minority residents of struggling cities. Further, to compel those residents to work in exchange for help, or even to make them attend programs that might boost self-reliance, was to violate their civil liberties.

The War on Poverty, motivated by such toxic ideas, transformed welfare from temporary assistance into a lifelong stipend with few strings attached. As everyone knows, welfare rolls then skyrocketed, increasing 125 percent from 1965 to 1970 alone, and an entrenched generational underclass of poor families emerged. Typically, they lived in dysfunctional public housing projects—many of them built as another battle in the War—that radiated blight to surrounding neighborhoods. The federal government created a series of huge initiatives, from Medicaid and Head Start to food stamps and school lunch programs, that spent billions of dollars trying to fight urban poverty. And then, to attack the "root causes" of poverty (whatever they were), the feds spent billions more on local social-services agencies, which ran ill-defined programs with vague goals like "community empowerment" that did nothing to alleviate poverty.

Despite years of effort and gargantuan transfusions of money, the federal government lost its War on Poverty. "In 1968 . . . 13 percent of Americans were poor," wrote Charles Murray in his unstinting examination of antipoverty programs, *Losing Ground*. "Over the next 12 years, our expenditures on social welfare quadrupled. And in 1980, the percentage of poor Americans was—13 percent."

These programs did, however, produce a seismic shift in the way mayors viewed their cities—no longer as sources of dynamism and growth, as they had been for much of the nation's history, but instead as permanent, sickly wards of the federal government. In fact, as the problems of cities like Cleveland and New York festered and metastasized, mayors blamed the sickness on the federal government's failure to do even more. Norquist recalled a U.S. Conference of Mayors session held in the aftermath of the 1992 Los Angeles riots. "There was almost a feeling of glee among some mayors who attended: finally the federal government would realize it had to do something for cities."

Even as tin-cup urbanism prevailed, however, some mayors began arguing for a different approach, based on the belief that cities could master their own futures. The nineties became an era of fruitful urban-policy experimentation. For instance, well before the federal welfare reform of 1996, various cities and counties, most notably Giuliani's New York and Norquist's Milwaukee (encouraged strongly by Wisconsin governor Tommy Thompson), not only set limits on welfare eligibility for the programs that they administered for the feds but also pursued a "work-first" policy that got able-bodied welfare recipients back into the workplace as swiftly as possible. Welfare rolls plummeted—in New York City, from 1.1 million in the early nineties to about 465,000 by 2001—and childhood poverty numbers decreased.

State and local legislators, often prodded by inner-city parents, also sought new ways to provide urban minority kids with a decent education. In Milwaukee, a former welfare mother, enraged that her children had no option other than the terrible public schools, helped push a school-voucher bill through the Wisconsin state legislature, letting disadvantaged students use public money to attend private schools. Most states passed laws enabling private groups to set up charter schools unencumbered by many of the union-backed rules found in public school systems, such as restrictions on firing lousy teachers. Today, some 4,300 charter schools, many in big cities, educate 1.2 million kids nationally—and most are performing, studies show, better than nearby public schools.

The era's most impressive urban reform improved public safety. Under Giuliani and his first police commissioner, William Bratton, New York City famously embraced Broken Windows policing, in which cops enforced long-dormant laws against public disorder, fostering a new climate of respect for the right of all citizens to use public spaces. The nineties' NYPD also introduced computer technology that tracked and mapped shifting crime patterns, so that police could respond quickly whenever and wherever crime spiked upward, and new accountability measures to ensure that commanders followed through. Crime in New York has plummeted 70 percent since the implementation of these reforms—double the national decline. Other cities that have adopted similar policing methods, from Newark to East Orange, New Jersey, to Raleigh, North Carolina, have had big crime turnarounds, too. As Newark mayor Cory Booker, who tapped an NYPD veteran as police director, noted about crime-fighting: "There are models in America, right in New York City, that show that this is not an issue of can we, but will we."

Obama may claim to be advancing a twenty-first-century agenda, but his ideas about combating poverty and aiding cities ignore the lessons of the nineties' reformers and remain firmly mired in the War on Poverty's vision of cities as victims. Nothing betrays his urban agenda's retrograde nature more than its Number One spending item: a big hike in funding for the Community Development Block Grant program. The candidate calls this relic of the War on Poverty "an important program that provides housing and creating [sic] jobs for low- and moderate-income people and places." In fact, the block grants are perhaps the most visible example of the failure of federal urban aid, plagued, as so much other War on Poverty spending was plagued, by vague goals, a failure to demand concrete results from the groups it funds, and a reputation for political patronage. CDBG money, amounting to some $110 billion over its history, has financed many projects that have zilch to do with fighting poverty—an opera house, a zoo, tennis courts, and historical restorations, for instance. A stark example of the program's failure to achieve its ostensible mission: Buffalo, the city that has received the most community redevelopment funding per capita, is economically worse off today than it was 40 years ago.

Nevertheless, CDBG spending is often invoked as evidence that the federal government is "doing something" about urban problems. This was the case in 1993, when the Clinton administration authorized a massive $430 million block grant to establish a loan fund to help Los Angeles recover from the previous year's devastating riots, as well as millions more to ameliorate "the underlying causes of the unrest." Within two years, though, a third of the companies that the loan money had financed had gone belly-up or fallen behind in payments, while two-thirds hadn't fulfilled their obligations to create new jobs in the city. As for the money aimed at "underlying causes," local officials merely spent it on yet more ineffective community groups.

Obama doubtless will claim that he can fix this kind of urban aid to make it more accountable, but the obstacles are great. The Bush administration, for instance, sought to junk most of the program and focus what remained on narrow projects with specific, measurable antipoverty goals. But congressional CDBG backers on both sides of the aisle, who insert millions of dollars in earmarks into it each year, derailed the reform.

Though Obama has supported some education reforms, such as charter schools, his plan for fixing urban schools by showering more federal money on them is another attempt to revive tin-cup largesse. In his signature education speech, Obama described visiting a high school outside Chicago that "couldn't afford to keep teachers for a full day, so school let out at 1:30 every afternoon," adding that "stories like this can be found across America." Later, he said: "We cannot ask our teachers to perform the impossible, to teach poorly prepared children with inadequate resources."

In fact, the U.S. has made vast investments in its public schools. According to a study by Manhattan Institute scholar Jay Greene, per-student spending on K–12 public education in the U.S. rocketed from $2,345 in the mid-1950s to $8,745 in 2002 (both figures in 2002 dollars). Per-pupil spending in many cities is lavish. In New York, huge funding increases dating to the late 1990s have pushed per-pupil spending to $19,000; across the river in Newark, state and federal aid has boosted per-pupil expenditures to above $20,000; and Washington, D.C., now spends more than $22,000 a year per student. Yet these urban school systems have shown little or no improvement. "Schools are not inadequately funded—they would not perform substantially better if they had more money," Greene observes. An Organisation for Economic Co-operation and Development study found that most European countries spend between 55 percent and 70 percent of what the U.S. does per student, yet produce better educational outcomes. If some urban school systems are failing children, money has nothing to do with it.

Obama also promises to invest heavily in the human capital of cities, seeking to forge a smarter, better-trained urban workforce. Yet here, too, his solutions look backward. His key proposal to help the chronically unemployable find work is simply to reauthorize the Workforce Investment Act of 1998. But politically connected insiders run many of the WIA's job-training initiatives, and waste is widespread. One Government Accountability Office study found that only about 40 percent of the $2.4 billion that the WIA designates for retraining dislocated workers actually went to the workers themselves; administrative costs gobbled up the rest. Even the money that reaches workers does little obvious good. In congressional testimony last year, a GAO official said, "We have little information at a national level about what the workforce investment system under WIA achieves."

Another big-ticket, War on Poverty–style item on Obama's agenda is to give cities more federal money to build "affordable" housing. Yet even as mayors warn about a critical shortage of housing for the poor and the middle class, many simultaneously claim that they are hemorrhaging population because of competition from suburbs—and that they should be lowering housing costs. Further, with foreclosures rising rapidly in some cities, cheap housing should be plentiful.

What explains this conundrum are the local policies that have helped make housing unaffordable. In a study called "The Planning Penalty," economist Randal O'Toole points out that half a century ago, when many cities were still gaining population, almost all of them boasted a healthy stock of affordable housing. Yet starting in the 1970s, cities began aggressively limiting and directing housing growth, enacting rules for minimum lot sizes and population density that produced significant cost increases for builders, who passed them on to consumers.

In Trenton, New Jersey, O'Toole estimates that the city-imposed planning penalty adds $49,000, or 17 percent, to the median cost of a home in a city where the population has shrunk from 130,000 in the 1950s to 85,000 today. In nearby Newark, a city pockmarked with empty lots that has lost some 170,000 residents, the planning penalty is $154,000, adding 41 percent to median home value. In New York, where Mayor Michael Bloomberg has committed $7.5 billion to build 165,000 units of affordable housing over ten years, the additional costs heaped on by government planning reach a whopping $311,000 per home. There's zero evidence that Obama understands the planning penalty at the heart of the affordable-housing shortage in many cities.

Obama and the U.S. Conference of Mayors also call for an increase in HOPE VI funding as a way of getting welfare families to stop thinking of public housing as a permanent entitlement. The HOPE VI program, launched in the early nineties, got cities to replace large projects with smaller communities where the subsidized poor would live among those who could afford market-rate housing. The hope was that the bourgeois values of those earning their way in life would somehow rub off on the recipients of housing subsidies, and that they would then move up and out. But because the program imposed no actual requirements on the poor, the effort failed. Research has shown that in cities like Memphis, where the poor have been dispersed to middle-class neighborhoods, crime is rising.

Judging by these and other Obama initiatives, an urban-reform agenda based on the bottom-up successes of the 1990s still awaits its national advocate. It would start from the notion that cities can indeed be masters of their own futures. It would encourage city self-empowerment, not victimhood. Above all, it would urge municipalities to build on the stunning urban-policy successes of the 1990s.

The feds could still, however, play a useful role in several areas. One would be to help cities attack the chronic unemployment and lack of achievement among the urban poor, especially men recently released from prison with neither the schooling nor the workplace experience to find jobs. Nationwide, some 700,000 prisoners finish their sentences every year. Lots go back to their home cities, where, aimless and unemployed, they reconnect with their old partners in crime, resume lawbreaking, and wind up back behind bars. Getting these former prisoners working not only might keep some from returning to crime; it could create a panoply of other benefits, including allowing the many who are absentee fathers to begin supporting the children they left behind when they went to jail.

Around the nation, one can find pockets of innovation on "prisoner reentry," often based on the same responsibility-building principles as welfare reform. Some of the most successful programs endorse a "work-first" philosophy that gets ex-cons back into the workplace under heavy supervision and mentoring, rather than simply offering them job training. Promising demonstration projects have used local churches and community groups to run job-placement services, provide mentors to former prisoners, and then help them discover community resources. Federal funds could help expand such programs. And Washington could bring the most successful ones to the federal prison system itself, since starting prisoners on the right path before they get back on the streets clearly cuts recidivism.

The feds should also tie funds to local governments' willingness to reform their own institutions for reintegrating ex-cons. For instance, in many cities, former offenders trying to find work face a forbiddingly complex municipal bureaucracy. But some places, like Newark, are trying to sweep away the red tape and create one-stop reentry centers for ex-prisoners, similar to those that New York created to help former welfare recipients find and keep employment.

Given the spectacular crime declines in New York and other cities that have followed its policing example, one might think that public safety is an area that requires no further federal role. But even as crime has begun rising again over the last few years, many police departments have shunned the new policing. Too many police officials and politicians continue to argue instead that factors beyond their control—from economic deprivation to cultural changes to bad federal policy—are to blame for crime. *Governing* magazine reports, for example, that Cleveland mayor Frank Jackson remains "skeptical about the ability of the police to solve the problem of crime, which he sees as deeply rooted in economic deprivation." Jackson told the magazine that "we look to the law, to the police, almost like an army that keeps everyone in check. That's a dangerous proposition." But a recent series of stories in the magazine *Cleveland Scene* with titles like "The Killing Fields" reveals the consequences of such an attitude: a city under siege, with murders rising 56 percent from 2005 through 2007.

The federal government can help advance performance-based police work by aiding departments in implementing NYPD-style policing, including purchasing the necessary technology for crime mapping. The city of East Orange, for instance, used state grants and criminal forfeiture money to pay for its $1.5 million technology upgrade. Federal grants would be contingent on departments' demonstrating that they are practicing active—not reactive—policing, using the same measurements that innovative departments now use to judge their officers' productivity, such as the number of directed patrols aimed at preventing crimes, suspicious-activity stops, and field interrogations per officer.

The deplorable state of many city school systems puts education reform high on the list of any twenty-first-century urban-reform agenda. Here, the federal government would provide incentives for states and municipalities to increase the education choices offered to students. Because many locales offer no public funding for building charter schools, for example, the feds might usefully help out. And Washington could tie federal education funding to requirements that states treat charter schools more equitably: in many states, charters get only a small portion of the per-pupil funding that regular schools receive. Federal education aid could also encourage states to lift their charter school caps. Today, roughly half the states limit the number of charter schools that they will authorize, one reason that about 365,000 students around the country remain on those schools' waiting lists.

The feds could also encourage schools to use curricula that work, especially to teach reading, since failing to learn to read in the early grades condemns many inner-city schoolchildren to fall permanently behind. The Bush administration admirably tried to prod school districts to adopt traditional, phonics-based programs, which are especially effective at educating minority students, the National Reading Panel concluded in 2000. But progressive educators who design curricula in local districts have continued to resist, favoring the ineffective but trendy "whole language" instruction touted by education schools.

As for increasing the amount of affordable housing, Washington could tie any housing aid to regulatory reforms that diminish or eliminate the construction caps and complex zoning requirements that drive up home prices. As Harvard economist Edward Glaeser has shown, Houston and several other cities impose so few government costs on housing—a planning penalty of $0, O'Toole finds—that quality housing gets built and sold at far lower prices than in more heavily regulated cities. Though Houston's economy boomed and its population grew by nearly 1 million during the 1990s, the price of housing there has increased at only slightly more than the rate of inflation.

At the same time, the federal government should transform its policies on housing for the poor by employing the same philosophy that drove welfare reform, placing limits on tenure in public housing and requiring residents to work toward lifting themselves out of poverty. A few cities are, in fact, transforming public housing by ending the idea that everyone has a right to it and by imposing strict requirements on tenants. In the mid-nineties, Atlanta began demolishing its giant projects, which once housed some 50,000 poor residents, and replaced them with smaller mixed-income, mixed-use projects built with both federal money and large contributions from private developers, who own and manage the housing. What attracted the private money was the promise from Atlanta's housing authority that these projects would be different: to live in them, all tenants between 18 and 65 had to have jobs or be in school so that eventually they could graduate out of public housing entirely. Whereas in the mid-1990s, less than 20 percent of the residents in Atlanta public housing were working, today it's about 70 percent. Federal housing authorities could adopt this model and urge other cities to follow it.

Finally, everyone agrees that the nation's transportation infrastructure, including that of its cities, is woefully inadequate for the twenty-first century. Both Obama and the U.S. Conference of Mayors—surprise!—blame the federal government for underinvesting in transportation infrastructure. But cities and states are equally at fault. Some have used past federal infrastructure grants simply to replace their own transportation money, which they've shifted to other, more politically popular uses. And cities have employed the tax-free municipal financing allowed by the federal tax code not to fund necessary improvements in transportation but to fund nonessential projects favored by politicians, like sports arenas and convention centers. Even when cities use this financing on transportation, it tends to be for big, expensive projects that rarely live up to ridership projections, like the massive $45 billion high-speed rail service that California pols have promoted to link Los Angeles and San Francisco—a service whose proponents, according to a Reason Foundation report, "wildly" overestimate potential ridership to justify the cost.

Boosting federal funding for such wasteful initiatives would only squander money. The federal government needs to reform its transportation priorities and push states and cities to do so, too, if we're to upgrade the nation's transportation infrastructure. That means rejecting dubious big-ticket projects and fashionable new modes of transportation, like light-rail systems, and spending federal funds on more sensible changes—helping cities to expand existing bus services, say, or to upgrade to cleaner vehicles. The federal government could also give cities incentives to build express toll roads that charge a premium for usage, alleviating congestion on free roads. And the feds should encourage local governments to use private contractors and private capital to build more of our public infrastructure, as countries ranging from France to the United Kingdom to China are now doing.

Obama's rise has put urban issues back into the presidential campaign for the first time in decades. But so far, the discussion that his candidacy has sparked is taking place largely among politicians, commentators, and interest groups whose view of cities hasn't moved on much from the War on Poverty. Implementing their policy ideas would simply expand the tin-cup urbanism that has kept so many cities in despair for so long. That's change we can do without.

2

Welfare Since Reform:
Is It Still Relevant?

Editor's Introduction

When President Bill Clinton signed the Personal Responsibility and Work Opportunity Act (PRWOA) into law on August 26, 1996, he declared that the legislation would "end welfare as we know it." In some ways, Clinton was right; the act represented a fundamental shift in the nation's method and goals in providing cash assistance to the poor. It replaced Aid to Families with Dependent Children (AFDC), the cash welfare system in place since 1935, with Temporary Assistance for Needy Families (TANF), which focused not on merely giving cash benefits to the poor and disadvantaged, but on ending their dependence on government assistance by helping them transition to the workforce and instilling in them a greater sense of pride and personal responsibility.

Passed at the height of the Great Depression as part of the Social Security Act, AFDC had been a matching-grant entitlement program, meaning that the federal government gave matching funds to each state for welfare payments to all those whom the state deemed eligible. As the program's cost and enrollment increased over the years—reaching its highest level of spending, adjusted for inflation, in 1976—many began to criticize AFDC for failing to offer incentives for people to find jobs, thereby creating an entire class of people who merely existed on welfare. For instance, there was no limit to how long a person could receive welfare benefits, and at that time minimum-wage jobs paid less than welfare. Ronald Reagan's derogatory reference to "welfare queens"—women who collected excessive welfare payments through fraud—during the 1976 presidential campaign served to stereotype welfare recipients in the minds of many as lazy and manipulative.

The TANF reforms sought to increase personal responsibility and encourage a transition back to work. One of the most significant changes was the program's five-year time limit for receiving welfare payments. Another major change was the requirement that recipients engage in a minimum number of work, or work-related, activities per week in order to receive continued benefits. No longer considered an entitlement, the state-run TANF programs were funded through block grants from the federal government based on a calculation of the number of needy families in each state. The block grants contained fewer spending restrictions, allowing state governments to fund additional programs, such as childcare or work-training services, if they so choose.

TANF—"one of the most closely watched social experiments in modern history," as Jason DeParle described it—was immensely controversial when it was passed. Fearing that it would leave impoverished children and families without any resources, a number of Democrats declared it an abomination and an insult to the poor. Some labeled it "anti-family," and predicted a massive increase in poverty rates and streets filled with begging children. Many Republicans, in contrast, hailed the legislation as an important bipartisan achievement and praised its emphasis on hard work and personal responsibility.

The actual effects of the 1996 reform efforts surprised both the program's supporters and opponents. Millions of people quickly left welfare. National and state employment rates rose and child poverty declined faster than anyone expected. The figures seemed impressive, even as many pointed out that they were at least in part due to an unusually strong national economy. Perhaps most shocking was the dramatic drop in welfare caseloads, which fell every year from 1994 to 2007. In 2007, TANF boasted only 4.1 million cases, the lowest figure since 1964. Supporters of the plan touted the results as evidence of the failure of the welfare state. Many who had initially criticized TANF joined the ranks of those who praised it as one of the greatest reforming efforts in history.

There were, however, many who interpreted the "accomplishments" of TANF in a different light. They blamed the program's constant focus on reducing enrollment for creating obstacles that discouraged needy families from applying and for using sanctions and punishments to push people off the rolls before they were ready. Critics also argued that the low unemployment rates touted by conservatives were misleading because they failed to account for what happened to welfare recipients after they left the rolls. Indeed, most took jobs that lacked benefits and provided wages that placed them below the poverty level. The subsequent increased enrollment in other social programs, such as food stamps and Medicaid, seemed to suggest that TANF was no longer serving those who needed it most.

In the Deficit Reduction Act of 2005, President George W. Bush reauthorized TANF until the year 2010. Among other changes, Bush's reauthorization plan increased work requirements for participants and narrowed the definition of "work activities." In addition, the bill provided increased funding for childcare services and grants for states to design programs that encouraged responsible fatherhood and healthy marriages. The American Recovery and Reinvestment Plan, signed by President Obama in February 2009, included increased funding for TANF and other state-run social initiatives for the poor in order to ease the impact of the economic recession.

The articles in this section explore the debate over the successes and failures of welfare reform and the program's role in the post-2000 economy. In the first article, "How Welfare Reform Worked," Kay S. Hymowitz compares the criticisms of TANF leveled by many Democrats in 1996 to the reality of the program's achievements. Hymowitz argues that an important reason for the success of welfare reform is that its goal has changed—from offering a financial safety net to changing a cultural attitude of dependency. Along similar lines, Ron Haskins and Isabel Sawhill contend in their article "Using Carrots and Sticks" that welfare reform succeeded because it offered the right incentives, requiring work in exchange for cash benefits. In contrast, in his piece "Is Welfare Working?" Jonathan Walters examines the program's main claim to success—the reduction in welfare roles— and concludes that the emphasis on caseload reduction has in many states led to both higher poverty rates and the creation of a permanent population of working poor.

In "Unfinished Business," Thomas Massaro argues that welfare reform should be revisited in light of the changing economic environment. In his article "Welfare Aid Isn't Growing as Economy Drops Off," Jason DeParle presents a troubling portrait of TANF's role in the current economic crisis, noting that as unemployment rates soar, state welfare rolls have continued to drop.

How Welfare Reform Worked*

By Kay S. Hymowitz
City Journal, Spring 2006

Welfare reform celebrates its tenth anniversary this year, and celebrates seems the right word. As most readers know, Temporary Assistance for Needy Families (TANF) ended the much-despised Depression-era federal entitlement to cash benefits for needy single mothers, replacing it with short-term, work-oriented programs designed and run by individual states. Its success has surprised just about everyone, supporters and naysayers alike.

So it seems a good time to remember the drama—make that melodrama—that the bill unleashed in 1996. Cries from Democrats of "anti-family," "anti-child," "mean-spirited," echoed through the Capitol, as did warnings of impending Third World-style poverty: "children begging for money, children begging for food, eight- and nine-year-old prostitutes," as New Jersey senator Frank Lautenberg put it. "They are coming for the children," Congressman John Lewis of Georgia wailed—"coming for the poor, coming for the sick, the elderly and disabled." Congressman William Clay of Missouri demanded, "What's next? Castration?" Senator Ted Kennedy called it "legislative child abuse," Senator Chris Dodd, "unconscionable," Senator Daniel Patrick Moynihan—in what may well be the lowest point of an otherwise miraculous career—"something approaching an Apocalypse."

Other Washington bigwigs took up the cry. Marion Wright Edelman of the Children's Defense Fund called the bill "national child abandonment" and likened it to the burning of Vietnamese villages. Immediately after President Clinton signed the bill, some of his top appointees quit in protest, including Edelman's husband, Peter, who let loose with an article in *The Atlantic Monthly* titled, "The Worst Thing Bill Clinton Has Done." No less appalled, the *Chicago Tribune* seconded Congresswoman Carol Moseley Braun's branding the bill an "abomination." And while in 2004 the *New York Times* lauded the legislation as "one of the acclaimed successes of the past decade," the editors seem to have forgotten that they were irately against it before they were for it, pronouncing it "draconian" and a "sad day for poor children."

It's worth recalling the outcry at this anniversary moment, not in order to have a gotcha-fest, pleasurable as such an exercise can be. The truth is that many of welfare reform's promoters were not spot-on in their predictions, either, and their expectations require some Monday-morning quarterbacking, too. But the apocalyptic scaremongering of reform opponents on the one hand, and the relative benignity of the bill's consequences on the other, prompt the obvious question: How is it that so many intelligent, well-intentioned people, including many experts who made up the late twentieth century's Best and Brightest, were so mistaken— mistaken not just in the way a weatherman who overestimates the strength of a snowstorm is mistaken, but fundamentally, intrinsically, and epistemologically wrong?

Before examining why so many people were wrong, let's look at exactly how they were wrong—an easy task, given the Everest of data on welfare reform's aftermath. TANF did not include a federal jobs program for the poor—though many wanted it to—but it has ended up being a WPA for social scientists, who have been busily crunching just about every number that happened to wander anywhere near a welfare recipient for the past ten years.

The most striking outcome has been the staggering decline in the welfare rolls, so large it has left even reform enthusiasts agog. At their peak in 1994—the rolls began to shrink before 1996, because many states had already instituted experimental reform programs—there were 5.1 million families on Aid to Families with Dependent Children, the old program. Almost immediately, the numbers went into freefall, and by 2004 they were down by 60 percent, to fewer than 2 million. A lot of reform opponents—the unreformed, so to speak—tried to chalk this up to the booming economy of the later 1990s. But according to former congressional staffer Ron Haskins, author of a history of the reform due out this fall, that doesn't make sense: in the 41 years between 1953 and 1994, he points out, the welfare rolls had declined only five times, and only once (between 1977 and 1979) for two years in a row. Compare that with the present case, when the rolls continued their fall even after a recession began in 2001, and when 2004 marked the tenth continuous year of decline.

Caseload declines are all well and good, but what caused opponents—and many proponents as well—to lose sleep was what would happen to women and their children once they left the dole. There were four chief concerns: First, would welfare leavers find jobs? Second, would they sink even deeper into poverty? Third, would their children be harmed? And fourth, would the states take advantage of the wide flexibility the bill gave them on implementation to join what many anticipated would be a "race to the bottom"?

So let's consider concern number one: Did women who left the rolls actually go to work? The answer is: more than almost anyone had predicted. According to one Urban Institute study, 63 percent of leavers were working in the peak year of

1999. True, some studies showed numbers only in the high fifties, but even these findings were much better than expected.

Nevertheless, a lot of skeptics still weren't biting. It was the luck of a boom economy, they said; just wait until the job market sours. Well, the recession came in 2001, and though it was no picnic, it was—once again—nothing like what had been feared. As of 2002, 57 percent of leavers continued to punch a time clock. That, the critics warned, was only because the first recipients to leave welfare were likely to be the most competent. Just wait until we're dealing with the most dysfunctional, those who have the most "barriers to employment"—from limited education or work experience to English-language deficiency or mental disability.

But even there the news was encouraging. The Urban Institute kept a close eye on the caseload composition in welfare reform's early years and found that the proportion of highly disadvantaged women was no greater in 1999 than in 1997. A 2003 study by June O'Neill and Anne Hill found a large increase in the employment of some of these women: for example, in 1992 only 31 percent of young single mothers who were high school dropouts were employed; by 2000, 50 percent had jobs. And none of this takes into account the women who under the previous regime might have gone on welfare but, after TANF, with its time limits and hassles, never did. The percentage of employed single mothers rose, in the years following reform, from 45 percent in 1990 to 62 percent in 2005—nearing the employment rate of their married counterparts.

What about concern number two—that welfare mothers would sink deeper into poverty? Shortly before TANF passed, the Urban Institute released a report, solicited by a wavering Clinton administration, warning that welfare reform could impoverish an additional 2 million people. Reform Jeremiahs waved the report around as scientific proof of their worst fears. Even if some welfare mothers did find jobs, they argued, they would merely be stocking shelves at Duane Reade or making hotel beds, the proverbial "dead-end jobs" that would leave them worse off than on the dole.

Though a lot of women did take low-paying service jobs, the unreformed got this one wrong, too. For one thing, they failed to consider the Earned Income Tax Credit, whose expansion in 1993 meant a 40 percent boost in annual earnings for a minimum-wage worker with two kids. Most leavers, though, were doing better than minimum wage. In 2002, the same Urban Institute that had predicted TANF disaster found that the median hourly wage for working former recipients was around $8 an hour. Moreover, O'Neill and Hill discovered that, just as with most other people, the longer recipients were in the job market, the more they earned; four years off welfare, only 4 percent of working single mothers—and only 8 percent of high school dropouts who were single mothers—were earning minimum wage or less.

As a result, most welfare leavers had more money than when they were on welfare. The poverty rate for single women with children fell from 42 percent in 1996 to 34 percent in 2002; before 1996, it had never in recorded history been below 40 percent. This was the first boom ever where poverty declined faster for that group than for married-couple families. Nor did leavers disdain their "dead-end jobs." Studies consistently found that ex-recipients who went on to become waitresses, grill cooks, and security guards took pride in being salarywomen.

Still, it's fair to say that while post-reform America did not look like Calcutta, it was no low-wage worker's paradise, either, especially as the economy weakened in late 2001. Ex-welfare mothers were still poorer than single mothers overall. Some who worked had less income than on welfare. Many were not working full-time, and an estimated 40 percent of those who left the welfare rolls returned later on. In 1999, close to 10 percent of leavers were "disconnected"—neither working nor on welfare nor supported by a working spouse. By the recession year of 2002, that number had risen to almost 14 percent. From the beginning, studies from the Children's Defense Fund and the Center for Budget and Policy Priorities warned of an increase in the number of families in deep poverty, and a steady stream of rumors claimed that soup kitchens and homeless shelters had crowds of ex-recipients clamoring at their doors.

But at least some of these warnings turned out to have been yet more crying wolf. Those who returned to the dole tended soon to find other means of support, getting a new job, signing up for disability or unemployment insurance, or turning to employed partners. As for deepening poverty, experts are often unsure what to make of official estimates of the income of the poorest of the poor, since they may have other sources of support than reported income. So they try to see if the income numbers conform to other measures. There was no evidence that single mothers were moving in with relatives, as you might expect if money were that tight. Harvard researchers Christopher Jencks and Scott Winship, neither of them avid reform supporters, found that, despite a big drop in the number of families using food stamps, worry among single mothers and kids about being able to afford the next meal declined between 1995 and 2000, and though such insecurity increased in the early 2000s, it never rose to pre-reform levels. Moreover, the lowest earners were buying more—spending money that, according to official numbers, they didn't have.

And that takes us to concern number three—the kids. Children were the unreformed's most lethal weapon: the image of kids starving in the streets, sleeping on grates, begging from strangers, and neglected and abused by desperate mothers, was enough to make the most robust reformer queasy. But the predicted Dickensian purgatory also turned out to be wrong. There may have been an increase in the number of children in foster care, but child abuse and neglect numbers are, depending on what measures you use, either unchanged or down.

More striking was what happened to rates of child poverty. They not only went down; by 2001, they hit all-time lows for black children. And though the numbers drifted up again during the recession, they were still lower than they had been pre-reform. On other measures, the young kids of ex-welfare moms are no worse off than under the old regime. Though some studies find lower achievement and more problem behavior among adolescents, the big picture doesn't show teen children in more trouble post-reform. After 1996, juvenile violence and teen pregnancy continued to go down, as they had since the early nineties.

As for the anti-reformer's final concern—the states' "race to the bottom"—that dog didn't bark, either. True, the enemies of reform might point at the 20-odd states that introduced a "family cap," which sought to stem illegitimacy by denying any increase in benefits to women who had another child while on welfare, and whose efficacy remains uncertain. But there's little question that the unreformed were wrong here as well—for the fourth time. The states were, if anything, nicer than the feds. No state barred cash benefits to teen mothers, though TANF permitted them to do so. Forty-seven states made it easier than the old system for leavers to keep some of their cash benefits when they first went to work. Many states, including New York, did away with TANF's five-year time limit for all intents and purposes by using state dollars to pick up the tab for those still on the dole at the time and deemed unable to work.

As caseloads declined, the states moved the federal money they would have spent on welfare benefits into work support—transportation, child care, and the like. In fact, under the states' management, welfare has morphed into an unprecedentedly generous work-support program. The real proof that the states were not the scoundrels that opponents had warned they would be came as Congress debated reauthorization after TANF expired in 2002. Reformers argued for even stricter federally mandated work requirements, while those who once warned that the states would engage in a race to the bottom demanded more state control.

This, then, is where we find ourselves today, ten years after reform: a record number of poor single mothers off the dole and the majority of them gainfully employed; less poverty among single mothers, especially black single mothers, as well as their kids; children adjusting well enough; and state governments taking care of their own. The situation is so far from what experts predicted that, as New York University political scientist Lawrence Mead has put it, it brings to mind the Sovietologists at the fall of the Soviet Union.

So how do reform opponents explain what went wrong when things went right? Some, like the team at the Children's Defense Fund, just continue to rejigger the numbers in dogged pursuit of evidence that the situation is much worse than anyone will admit. Others have been self-reflective. In 2004, Andrew Cherlin, one of the nation's top family scholars, gave a revealing speech to the annual meeting of the American Sociological Association, in which in light of his own study's benign findings, he tried to reassess his own earlier opposition to reform. "How should progressives respond to what we know so far about welfare reform and children?" he asked. "By progressives, I mean leftist/liberal and feminist scholars and observers, who, based on past experience, probably constitute 80 to 90 percent of this audience." His answer suggests some serious soul-searching. "[T]here may be something to the idea that long-term dependency on public assistance is detrimental," he conceded, though he had always "rejected this idea out of hand prior to 1996." Poor mothers "derive a basic dignity" from work. In fact, he continued, "as a result of what I have seen, I now think the term "dead-end job" is a label that often doesn't fit the perceptions of low-income workers; and I will not use it again."

It was a thoughtful admission, yes, but only a start. "Progressives"—a term that, given the present context, seems due for retirement—need to go much deeper than that. It is not simply that they were wrong in making a few isolated predictions; after all, there were bound to be legitimate questions about how to transform welfare and about what would happen afterward. It's that those predictions rested on a scaffold of moldy assumptions not just about poverty but about what kind of country we live in, how human beings decide to live their lives, and what role government plays in those decisions—in other words, about our politics in the deepest sense. "At times," Jason DeParle writes in his fine book *American Dream*, as he describes the debate in Washington in 1996, "it seemed the very idea of America was on trial."

Consider the assumptions of these "progressive pessimists," as we'll call them, about what motivated American opposition to welfare. Their answer appears to be: greed laced with a hefty shot of malice. They repeatedly compared what they viewed as the paltry social welfare spending of the United States with that of Western Europe, whose large welfare states supposedly reflected the citizenry's generosity. Americans, they said, were either indifferent or—some on the extreme Left argued—hostile toward the less fortunate. Americans want to "punish" or "scapegoat" the poor. They enjoy "the politics of meanness," a phrase coined by then-*Times* columnist Anna Quindlen and repeated persistently by the liberal commentariat. This view led to the expectation that states would "race to the bottom." After his intemperate *Atlantic* article, Peter Edelman warned that ending the federal entitlement meant that states could "do anything they want"—and what they wanted, implicitly, was to let the poor starve.

Progressive pessimists were blind to the promise of reform partly because they believed that the American discomfort with welfare was really a mask for racism. The term "progressive" may imply forward thinking, but in many ways the pessimists are still living in George Wallace's America. Welfare recipients were, and are, disproportionately black: African Americans totaled about 37 percent of the welfare rolls in 1996, though they were only about 12 percent of the population. If Americans didn't like welfare, pessimists reasoned, it was because they didn't like black people. Wags referred to welfare reform as "racism in drag" and to workfare as "slavefare." A perfect example of the Left's assumption that racist motives prompted welfare reform is a 1999 book called *Why Americans Hate Welfare*, by Yale political scientist Martin Gilens. Far from being mean-spirited, Americans are actually a fairly generous people, Gilens argued. If they hate welfare, it's not because they are tight; it's because they don't want to help black folks. With the help of a subliminally racist media, they look at black welfare recipients as lazy freeloaders, just as they did in the Jim Crow South. That Gilens wrote his book just as the Americans who hated welfare were helping to push black child poverty rates to their lowest levels in history seems not to have caused him a moment's cognitive dissonance.

Progressive pessimists were especially gloomy when it came to the American economy. You can't blame them for not foreseeing the economic exuberance of the second half of the 1990s; few did. Less defensible was their deep-rooted assumption that poverty was "structural," as permanent a part of the American scene as the Appalachian Mountains. Economic growth might be useful to the Mercedes-driving rich but not to the poor, they asserted. No matter how strong the economy, there still wouldn't be enough jobs, employers wouldn't hire welfare mothers, and those who did would offer them only the most demeaning and temporary work.

From this vantage point, any talk about "personal responsibility" was only more evidence of racially tinged victim-blaming. Nothing distinguishes progressive pessimists from their pro-reform counterparts more than their attitudes toward self-sufficiency. For the pessimists, poverty in America was so severe, and dead-end jobs so demoralizing, that they almost invariably shattered the individual will (and, incidentally, led to such social pathology as child abuse). That's why, if manufacturing jobs moved out of the ghetto, the pessimists explained, the poor could not be expected to move where there were more opportunities—though throughout the eighties and nineties, millions of poor immigrants were doing just that.

For reformers, on the other hand, there was much to learn from "immigrant optimism," as it's sometimes called. People are capable of far more resourcefulness and resilience than welfare recipients had been given a chance to show, they contended. This understanding was one reason why Bill Clinton rejected the advice of most of his advisors and signed welfare reform in August 1996. "I've always known poor folks," he told Jason DeParle in an interview quoted in *American Dream*. "I've just never thought they were helpless." DeParle's own research reached the same conclusion.

Social science tended to reinforce the dark assumptions of progressive pessimists. After all, as Andrew Cherlin's speech to his audience of sociologists suggests, the pessimists dominate the research community. The handful of pro-reformers doing poverty research didn't get much respect, until the Republicans took over Congress in 1994. According to a 2000 article on the politics of welfare reform by Diana Zuckerman, a onetime Democratic congressional staffer, House and Senate Democrats were working under "very liberal leadership of many congressional committees," who were used to getting their numbers from groups like the Children's Defense Fund and the Center for Budget and Policy Priorities. Staffers tended to dismiss the very different findings of more conservative experts as "ideological," an irony that would be laugh-worthy if its consequences hadn't been so dire.

But bias is not the most important reason that social-science research supported the pessimists and failed to predict accurately what would happen after welfare reform. In poverty research, labor economists—credited with having the most sophisticated measurements—are key players. But labor economists have a limited framework for analyzing human motivation and almost never deal with actual poor people, a combination that leaves them vulnerable to the cause-correlation confusion that so bedevils social science. Worse, what they can't measure—and what therefore never entered into progressive thinking—is the key role that values, or culture, plays in making people into productive citizens who go to school, do their homework, plan their lives, and work to support themselves and their families.

Human beings tend to do pretty much what they are expected to do. When the culture expects self-sufficiency, people will try to achieve it. When the culture sends mixed messages about self-sufficiency, as it did during the old welfare regime—particularly to the minority poor—some will not try to become self-sufficient. Experts couldn't calculate that simple dynamic, since fuzzy notions like values, norms, and culture are not easily quantifiable. The economists assumed that people were mere rational calculators, maximizers of self-interest, who would naturally try to be financially independent if the optimal incentives were in place. Moreover, used to drawing conclusions from small, experimental programs, they could not model the cultural effects of the large-scale policy shift that occurred in 1996.

The architects of TANF certainly relied on economic incentives, including the definitive one—no benefits after five years. But the bill's sticks and carrots added up to something greater than the sum of their parts. In a variety of ways—ending the federal welfare entitlement, forgoing the customary escape hatch of training programs in lieu of jobs—it was an unambiguous expression of a social consensus about work and self-reliance. The idea was not to get people to respond to particular inducements. It was much bigger than that: to try to get them to change their orientation toward life.

The impact on the ground was unmistakable. Sharon Hays, the sociologist author of *Flat Broke with Children: Women in the Age of Welfare Reform* and no friend of TANF, describes a bureaucracy completely transformed by the new law. With the help of an influx of federal money and firm leadership, local offices spiffed up their waiting rooms, hung inspirational banners proclaiming perseverance, success, and determination, and became job-search and -support centers. "Like caseworkers, almost all welfare recipients noticed the public enthusiasm for reform signaled by all the new programs, the influx of federal dollars, and the surge of media coverage that occurred in the first years after implementation," Hays writes. In other words, through TANF, the culture spoke, and poor women listened.

All of this might seem to lead to the conclusion that welfare reform has been a triumph for conservative thinking. That would be overstating things. TANF was never simply about ending welfare dependency. As part of a larger bill called the Personal Responsibility and Work Opportunity Reconciliation Act (PRWORA), it was designed to improve the lives of the formerly dependent more broadly by nudging them toward middle-class life.

The Left always thought of moving up as a matter of money, not behavior: if people earned a middle-class income, they believed, middle-class conduct and aspiration would be sure to follow. Conservatives tend to see it the other way around: middle-class mores are necessary for economic success. If people adopt bourgeois habits and ambitions, they will work hard, save, and plan, and eventually have the money to make a down payment on a house or pay parochial school tuition. In the case of PRWORA, supporters took this idea a bridge too far. They imagined the work ethic as the engine that would carry all other virtues in its train. Jobs would bring discipline to the lives of poor single mothers and transform them and their children. Work would turn them into bourgeois strivers.

And you do hear stories that seem to support that theory. Take Jewel, one of the three protagonists of Jason DeParle's *American Dream*. After failing repeatedly, she finally got her GED after the book came out, and is now studying for a nursing degree, even while she holds down a full-time job. She is still with her boyfriend of ten years, and he, in turn, has kept straight in the six years since he was released from prison, working during most of that time. Though they haven't married, they are raising their son together, pooling their money, and behaving in most respects like a married couple—helping, as DeParle told me, to "stabilize and encourage each other."

But taken as a whole, you'd have to conclude that welfare reform has not been the extreme makeover that supporters had sought. And the reason is that it has barely touched the single-mother problem. Reform optimists predicted that by heightening women's self-respect and belief in their future, work would make them more marriage-minded. "Women, realizing welfare won't support them, may begin to make better choices: demanding more from the men in their lives, delaying childbirth, teaming up with breadwinners," journalist Mickey Kaus theorized. Reformers also hoped that work requirements would act as a deterrent: girls seeing their mothers and older sisters juggling a low-paying job, an apartment, and children, all without a husband's help, would shun such a life.

Moreover, PRWORA had provisions to attack the single-parent problem in a variety of ways, from cracking down on deadbeat dads to abstinence education, experimental marriage-education programs, and bonuses to states that brought down their out-of-wedlock birthrate. The act was supposed to have a clear message: children should be born to married parents who are responsible for raising them.

Perhaps without PRWORA, things would have been worse. After rising steeply for three decades, the increase in the rate of out-of-wedlock births did slow around 1994. Robert Rector of the Heritage Foundation points out that if the pre-reform trend line had continued, 42 percent of all babies would be born fatherless today; instead, the number is about 35 percent. "Something different happened in the 1990s that didn't happen in Europe," where illegitimacy rates continued their inexorable climb, he observes. Moreover, the marriage rate among black Americans was substantially higher in 1998 than the trend line from 1960 to 1990 would have predicted. The number of poor couples who were cohabiting at the time of their babies' birth also rose. Still, a slowdown in the spread of illegitimacy and more shacking up among poor men and women—a notoriously fickle domestic arrangement—are not what optimists had in mind.

Ending welfare dependency, then, is not likely to turn poor mothers and fathers into child-centered soccer parents. Though researchers haven't found that reform has had any adverse effect on children, they haven't found much positive impact, either. Jason DeParle's book and others that look at the lives of poor families after reform give a pretty good idea why. Just because a woman has to be at a job at 8 each morning doesn't mean that her child's father has become a paragon. For that matter, just because she's following the dictates of an alarm clock doesn't mean that she is envisioning a better life for her children.

In Adrien Nicole LeBlanc's *Random Family,* the boyfriend of one working ex-welfare mother minds her children while he bags crack cocaine in the kitchen. All three of the children of one of DeParle's protagonists, Angie, have quit high school. Her eldest son describes his aunt's boyfriend, a drug dealer, as his role model. As a teenager, her daughter began spending time with a family friend who happens to be a prostitute. When DeParle questions Angie about why she doesn't try to discourage the friendship, the mother of three huffs, "I'm not supposed to let my kids visit her 'cause that's her chosen profession? . . . You don't judge people about stuff like that!" Today Angie's daughter is 22, with no husband, two children, and a job as a checkout clerk. It's better than being on welfare, sure, but not much for the history books.

What reformers especially didn't factor into their marriage visions was that PRWORA, like so much of American social welfare policy, had little to say to the prospective husbands. While experts sometimes overstate the shortage of marriageable men, it is true that employment levels for men with a high school education have been declining since the 1980s. The situation is especially dire for blacks. At the same time that poor black single mothers were setting off to work in record numbers, the employment rates of their would-be husbands barely budged, despite the boom economy of the late 1990s and despite their rising education levels. (These numbers don't even take into account the 21 percent of non-college-educated young black men who are incarcerated.) By 2000, employment rates for black men were around 25 percent lower than for whites and Hispanics.

Put all of this together—low-income single mothers, idle (and sometimes imprisoned) men, children with no vision of a way out (and no help from their schools on that score)—and you get a group only slightly different from the welfare families we had before: the struggling, working-single-mother family. So far, it seems better than its predecessor. Life in many inner-city neighborhoods has improved noticeably from its nadir in the late 1980s and early 1990s. Paul Jargowsky and Isabel Sawhill recently published a paper called "The Decline of the Underclass," showing a sharp decline in census "underclass tracts"—areas defined by their thick concentration of underclass behaviors, including welfare dependency, dropping out of school, and crime. If neighborhoods are improving, part of the reason, though it's impossible to calculate how much, is welfare reform. But at least as big a reason is that many of the most dangerous people have been sent away, so crime has gone down.

So what do policymakers do next? First, TANF, which Congress has just reauthorized for five years only—after several years of dickering over child care and work rules—needs to become a permanent fixture of American policy. The Left will always use reauthorization debates as a stage to push for more funding for day care and a higher minimum wage—policies that do nothing to change the fragile cultural landscape in which the single-mother family struggles. To make that transformation, more men have to become attached to work and to marriage, rather than to crime or prison. However, unlike with women who were dependent on welfare checks, policymakers have fewer levers to change the culture of unskilled, uneducated men.

As for the revival of wedlock, aside from as yet unproven marriage education programs that will reach only a small number of people anyway, social policy can play only a limited role. What's needed instead is a blitz of marriage talk from the churches, from the black leadership, from the political class, from celebrities like Bill Cosby, from radio and television spots—from anyone and everyone who might get the ear of the welfare population. This campaign will not lead poor mothers and their boyfriends to surge into wedding chapels; most never planned to raise children together, and they have pretty dismal long-term prospects. Rather, the marriage blitz needs to speak to a new generation of young people still able to rethink the possible outlines of their lives.

Policy has given the culture a nudge, but now the culture has to change itself.

Using Carrots and Sticks[*]

By Ron Haskins and Isabel Sawhill
American Prospect, May 2007

In the last decade, we have seen that an effective approach to reducing poverty requires changes in personal behavior as well as government support. Further, we have learned that by judiciously applying policies that demand and then reward good behavior—what might be called carrots-and-sticks policies—we can induce and maintain the behavior that leads to reduced poverty. Reviewing the record of the past decade suggests the principles that should guide future efforts.

During the 1960s, child poverty fell by more than half, to 14 percent. In the subsequent three decades, however, child poverty drifted upward in an uneven pattern, never again reaching the low level achieved in 1969. This is a surprising and discouraging record.

A major cause of the huge decline in poverty of the 1960s was an economy that grew 35 percent in per capita gross domestic product, giving rise to President Kennedy's famous observation that "a rising tide lifts all boats." Although the American economy has grown at a more stately pace since the 1960s, each subsequent decade has nonetheless seen substantial growth of more than 20 percent in per capita GDP—plenty of raw material, one would think, to continue the poverty reduction that distinguished the '60s. But the 24 percent GDP growth of the 1970s saw poverty fall by a mere 5 percent, and the 23 percent GDP growth of the '80s saw poverty actually increase by 12 percent. Clearly, a rising tide was not lifting all boats. The second half of the '90s, however, once again saw strong economic growth accompanied by the fastest and deepest decline in child poverty since the '60s.

WHY DID POVERTY DECLINE?

Three trends tell us a lot about the causes of poverty and show us why a growing economy has not been more effective in reducing it. First, growth of wages at the bottom of the distribution (the 10th percentile) declined during the 1980s and the first half of the '90s, rising again only after 1996.

Trend in Real Hourly Wages

. . . at selected points in the U.S. wage distribution, 1979-2003

95TH PRECENTILE

MEDIAN WAGE

10TH PRECENTILE

1979   2003

Source: Economic Policy Institute

High Employment. Stagnant or falling wages at the bottom of the distribution make reducing poverty difficult. By contrast, tight labor markets, as signaled by low unemployment rates, contribute to both rising wages and falling poverty rates.

Consider the record: Wages rose and poverty fell during the 1960s, when unemployment averaged 4.8 percent and fell as low as 3.5 percent. But as wages fell or were stagnant during the '70s and '80s, when unemployment skyrocketed to average 6.2 percent and 7.3 percent, respectively, poverty rose or was stagnant. Only when tight labor markets returned after the mid-'90s—when unemployment fell to an average of 4.8 percent between 1995 and 2000—did wages once again rise and poverty fall. Mere economic growth will not necessarily lead to reduced poverty rates. Apparently, tight labor markets accompanied by rising wages are required to effectively fight poverty.

Family Factors. A second factor putting substantial upward pressure on poverty was changes in family composition. The poverty rate for mother-headed families is usually four or five times the rate for married-couple families. So, other things being equal, any rise in the share of children living in female-headed families will increase poverty.

Beginning in the 1960s, Americans perfected every known method of casting children into single-parent families. Marriage rates fell, divorce rates increased until the 1980s, and non-marital birth rates exploded until a third of all babies (and nearly 70 percent of black babies) were born outside marriage. As a result, between 1970 and 2004, the percentage of children living in a female-headed family increased from 12 percent to 28 percent. It's hard to fight poverty when more and more children are in families of the type that are most likely to be poor.

Education. Poor educational achievement is a third reason poverty has been stagnant. Education has always been important in accounting for economic success, but most analysts agree that recent decades—because of globalization, technological change, and trade—have seen increased payoff to education. One of the most important changes in the American economy for those interested in fighting poverty is the decline of high-paying jobs suited to workers with a high-school education or less. Workers without a high-school diploma are twice as likely to be poor as those with one, and three times as likely to be poor as workers with some college education. The Educational Testing Service estimates that nearly one-third of students drop out of school before graduating. Moreover, despite waves of educational reform, the reading and math achievement of students from poor and low-income families has been virtually flat for three decades.

So there are at least three raging rivers against which those who would fight poverty must struggle: low wages, the rise of single-parent families, and lousy education. To offset these currents, the nation has spent an increasing amount of money on government programs to fight poverty. Between 1968 and 2004, the total of inflation-adjusted federal and state spending on means-tested programs (those that specify an income level above which individuals or families cannot qualify for benefits) increased from $89 billion to $585 billion—all without reducing poverty below its late-1960s level.

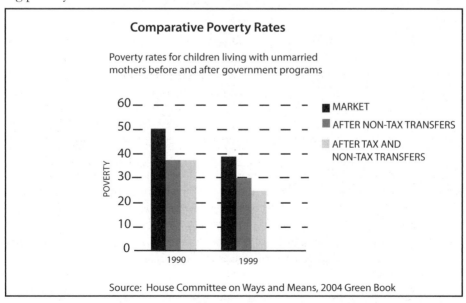

Source: House Committee on Ways and Means, 2004 Green Book

The net impact of these factors—economic growth, wages, family composition, education, and government spending—is high child-poverty rates. It is especially notable that the three factors over which individuals have full or partial control—work, family composition, and education—were either stable or moved in the wrong direction. Until recently, millions of Americans failed to work, many languishing on welfare. Millions also decided to have children outside marriage, to avoid marriage, or to divorce. And millions of young people refused to apply themselves during their school years, eventually either dropping out of school or graduating with low reading and math skills.

THE ROLE OF WELFARE REFORM

Yet the mid-1990s saw a dramatic example of how public policy can both help individuals improve their choices and reward them for doing so, namely the 1996 welfare-reform Law, passed on a huge bipartisan vote in Congress and signed by Democratic President Bill Clinton. Perhaps the law's single most notable feature was that it made cash welfare contingent on individuals working or preparing for work. Individuals who did not meet work requirements had their cash benefit reduced, and in most states even terminated.

In addition, the law limited federal benefit receipt to five years for any given parent. The work requirements, reduction of benefits for those who did not work, and five-year time limit all served as sticks that encouraged or forced parents on welfare to work. Much to everyone's surprise, mothers went to work by the hundreds of thousands, and the welfare rolls declined by more than 60 percent, far more than ever before. But most important, poverty among children in single-parent families fell by 30 percent, reaching its lowest level ever. Not surprisingly, given the high proportion of black children living in female-headed families, black child poverty also reached its lowest level ever.

RAISING REWARDS OF WORK

Government-imposed work requirements were an important part of this welcome decline in child poverty. But work is only half the picture. Most welfare mothers, who typically can qualify for jobs paying about $8 per hour, were not able to earn enough money to bring their families out of poverty. Realizing that financial payoffs to work were an important part of helping low-income families, federal and state governments, over a period of more than two decades, created and expanded programs specifically designed to help low-income working families. These included Medicaid health insurance, child care, food stamps, and above all, the Earned Income Tax Credit (EITC), a taxpayer-provided wage subsidy that could give working parents up to $4,000 in cash (in 1996).

Census Bureau data for children living with their single mothers present a clear picture of why this new system of earnings from increased work effort supplemented by benefits from work-support programs led to such a dramatic reduction in child poverty. In the second chart, the bar graphs on the left are for 1990; those on the right are for 1999. The first graph in each set shows the poverty rate that characterized these families based only on their market income before any government payments—poverty in the state of nature, so to speak. Here it can be seen that increased work by mothers between 1990 and '99 led to a huge 11 percentage point reduction in poverty. When government cash and in-kind benefits other than those delivered through the tax code are added, poverty falls 13 percentage points in 1990. But poverty also falls by 9 percentage points in 1999, demonstrating that working families are receiving work-support benefits to supplement their earnings to further reduce market poverty. Adding tax benefits, primarily the EITC, does not reduce poverty at all in 1990, but reduces it another 5 percentage points in 1999. The combination of work and work supports reduces poverty a full 12 percentage points—or by about 4.5 million people—more in 1999 than in 1990. It was the stick of welfare reform that induced mothers to leave welfare for work; it was the carrot of work-support benefits that supplemented the mothers' earnings and led to substantial reductions in poverty.

There are lots of good ideas for further reductions in poverty—improving and expanding preschool education; improving the public schools, especially for students from poor families; reducing nonmarital births; increasing marriage rates; encouraging savings; and helping poor young men improve their earnings—but the decline of poverty among female-headed families in the 1990s illustrates the principles that should guide the nation's efforts. The first is that individuals must change their behavior—or the nation will not be able to substantially reduce poverty. The second is that policy-makers should seek out policies that encourage or demand responsible behavior, and then use public dollars to reward it.

Is Welfare Working?[*]

By Jonathan Walters
Governing Magazine, February 2008

Twelve years ago, Bill Clinton and the U.S. Congress ended "welfare as we know it." Gone was the idea of an open-ended entitlement for those mired in poverty. In its place came Temporary Assistance for Needy Families and the notion that families could—and should—work their way out of their impoverished straits.

More than a decade into the change—including major revisions that were part of a 2005 reauthorization of TANF—the question today is not so much whether TANF works but whether welfare as we now know it still matters. As with any program that profoundly changes its ground rules, the original TANF and its subsequent 2005 revisions have unleashed a series of fallouts—some surprising, others not so. While they have relieved pressure on the program itself—welfare caseloads have fallen dramatically—there has been a notable and increasingly sharp uptick in the demand for services in other parts of the safety net.

"We really don't do much cash assistance to families anymore," says Sharon Hirsch, an assistant director in the Durham County (North Carolina) Department of Social Services. That money, she reports, is now going mostly to child-only cases where no parent and no work requirement is involved and to child care for the few families on the rolls. Meanwhile, welfare spending is dwarfed by what the county is now spending on other supplemental assistance programs, such as food stamps and Medicaid.

That trend has led many to wonder whether TANF has essentially run its course and whether welfare as we've come to know it is now a thing of the past, supplanted by a network of different safety net programs supporting the working poor.

THE BIG NUMBERS

The single most stunning effect of the 1996 TANF law has been the winnowing of welfare caseloads. Even in cities such as New York that had long hosted large numbers of people in need of assistance, caseloads tumbled and remain at historic lows. Since TANF went into effect, they are down nationally between 50 and 90 percent, depending on the city or state.

The reductions have been impressive, but have people been better off under the new regime? There is considerable evidence that many have. Through the late 1990s, poverty among single-parent families fell by 30 percent. Black-child poverty reached its lowest level in history.

A strong economy played a key role in driving down poverty rates during that period, says Isabel Sawhill, senior fellow and director of economic studies with the Brookings Institution. But, she notes, so did welfare reform, which, besides emphasizing work, gave states the flexibility to help clients with things such as child care, transportation, clothing and whatever else a family needed in order to get on its feet.

Another factor behind improved financial circumstances was the federal earned income tax credit, which could add thousands of dollars to a low-wage worker's income. With a good package of work supports, including a state as well as a federal EITC, Medicaid, food stamps and child care, a state could, says David Hansell, commissioner of New York State's Department of Temporary and Disability Services, "double someone's actual income up to 200 percent of the poverty level."

That's the good news. In the past few years, things have not been going quite as well. Caseloads aren't escalating back up but, says Robert Doar, commissioner of New York City's Human Resources Administration, "we've stalled." There's also evidence that the welfare program has become a more punitive system—one geared to pushing people off the rolls rather than helping them become employed and self-sufficient. And the cost of that approach is showing up in increased use of food stamps, Medicaid and other safety net programs.

THE SECOND STAGE

The word "stalled" is now being applied in more and more places. In most states, caseloads have either stabilized or are trending slightly upward.

One reason is that the easy cases have been washed out of the system. Those who were essentially work-ready—they just needed a little push and a little extra help—are off the rolls. Now the caseload is made up of those who have more serious and numerous barriers to employment. In New York, for instance, only about one-third of the state's caseload has as much as a high school education. Many are immigrants who don't speak English.

According to a recent Urban Institute report, more than half of all post-2005 TANF recipients have at least two significant barriers to work. "The people coming for assistance now," says Kevin McGuire, who oversees TANF in Maryland, "are people with physical, mental and emotional problems."

This more challenging cohort has distilled out at a particularly bad time: The economy has softened considerably since the late 1990s and is showing signs of getting worse. On top of that, Congress and the Bush administration imposed new rules in 2005 that reset the odometer on work participation rates and narrowed the definition of what states could count as work activity.

In other words, a dozen years into the boldest experiment in social policy in generations, states are finding that new federal policies and the national economy are lining up against a harder-to-serve group of clients. In the face of the twin challenges, states have—to varying degrees—been looking at two kinds of responses. One is to find ways to accommodate those with multiple barriers to work. The other is to toughen up the use of sanctions when individuals either fail or refuse to live up to the new work requirements.

Two years ago, for example, New York City launched a program, WeCare, to help clients with multiple barriers to work. Those who need extra help are steered to one-stop service providers who have contracted with the city to perform a full assessment that takes into consideration everything from an individual's physical and mental health to his or her social circumstances. The same contractor is then responsible for coming up with a plan to get the client work-ready, implementing that plan and doing a job placement. If a client is clearly incapable of getting and holding a job, that person is diverted out of the welfare program and into more permanent assistance, including the federally funded Supplemental Security Income program.

In Pennsylvania, programs aimed at working with harder-to-place welfare clients started as early as 2001, with the state's Maximizing Participation Program. The program targeted TANF recipients who had been exempted from work requirements because of some mental or physical disability. As a matter of policy, MPP favors continued education over work where appropriate and tries to engage those with multiple barriers in alternative work activities. As in New York City, if clients are simply incapable of further progress, MPP tries to divert them out of TANF altogether and into state or federal assistance.

TOUGH LOVE

There has always been the threat and use of sanctions. Those clients who don't live up to work requirements could be hit with penalties, which include everything from a gradual ratcheting down of benefits to an immediate and complete cutoff of benefits. But the use of sanctions has become an even more prominent feature of the program in the wake of the 2005 reauthorization, which changed the welfare-to-work landscape in two fundamental ways.

As part of the original 1996 bargain, states were granted more flexibility in how they handled welfare but had to achieve a 50 percent work participation rate for single-parent cases and 90 percent for households with two parents. States hit those percentages with ease early on, and then were allowed to continue using those gains to calculate participation rates for the life of TANF I. Under the 2005 reauthorization rules, Congress reset the clock—states would have to meet participation rates anew and, as it turns out, among a tougher-to-place clientele. At the same time, the new rules tightened up the definition of "work," disallowing activities—such as work-readiness classes—that in the past could be counted as having a job.

Critics of the new body of rules say that the most pernicious effect is that it has nudged state and local welfare workers back toward a focus on compliance as an outcome, rather than actually helping people work toward permanent independence, making TANF a meaner program that discourages people from signing up for it in the first place. "The system has become totally punitive," argues Evelyn Ganzglass with the left-leaning Center on Law and Social Policy. "We were moving in the right direction for nine years and then everything changed."

The trend—for states to be more aggressive about diverting or sanctioning people—is particularly troubling, critics say, because studies suggest that those enrolled in TANF are better off than otherwise-eligible families that either have been sanctioned off TANF or never signed up in the first place.

Those who argue that welfare today has reverted to more of a sanction-driven numbers game hold up Georgia as Exhibit A. TANF caseloads have declined "consistently and substantially" since 2004, according to a study by Mathematica Policy Research. Meanwhile, during the same time period, the state's work-participation rates for TANF recipients have skyrocketed from around 11 percent to nearly 70 percent.

That sounds impressive, except the gains in the percentage of those participating in work have been won not by placing more TANF recipients in work but by pushing down total caseloads. According to the Mathematica report, staff in Georgia "may be dissuading families from ever applying for TANF." In the wake of the state's aggressive push on work participation, the number of adults on TANF in Georgia has collapsed from a high of more than 50,000 at any one time to around 3,000 today.

Critics of the approach, such as Alan Essig, executive director of the Georgia Budget and Policy Institute, argue that the result is more Georgians living in poverty, not fewer. He notes that as participation in TANF has tumbled in Georgia—by 83 percent between 2002 and 2006—poverty rates have increased from 12 percent to just over 14 percent. At the same time, participation in other public assistance programs has gone up, increasing 160 percent in the case of food stamps and 15 percent for Medicaid.

The two trends taken together suggest that what Georgia has achieved through its aggressive stance on TANF is not a class of citizens working to become financially independent but rather the creation of a group of working poor, who seem to be slipping further behind and who require increasing amounts of other types of public assistance to survive.

If that's the case, it's still better than being on TANF, argues Donna Gunter, TANF unit manager for Georgia. "We operate on the assumption that welfare is not good enough for any family," she says. "If you're on welfare, we're maintaining you below the poverty level, so caseworkers are trying very hard to get families to see employment and other options that are available to them."

The overall trend in welfare that is on display in Georgia—a small but still-poor cadre of citizens stuck in poverty—appears to be one that is taking place in quite a few states and localities. Even states that aren't being accused of force-them-off-TANF tactics are seeing TANF participation among adults stay low, while food stamp and Medicaid participation and costs swing upward.

For Wade Horn, who helped craft the 2005 reauthorization legislation when he was assistant secretary for children and families at the U.S. Department of Health and Human Services, having people leave the cash-welfare program and become high users of other programs isn't a bad thing. "The framers of reform," he says, "didn't say people were going to leave welfare and their first job would put them into the middle class."

But the change in safety-net dymanics has been so pronounced in some places that TANF as a family welfare program has almost become irrelevant. In Durham County, Sharon Hirsch reports, the number of cases that are subject to work requirements has dwindled to around 100 in any given month.

Hirsch has seen welfare reform play out since before 1996. Under Governor Jim Hunt, North Carolina was granted a waiver to become an early adopter of the "work-first" approach to welfare. Counties were on the front line of that reform—North Carolina is one of about a dozen states where welfare is county-administered—and Hirsch at the time was executive director of the North Carolina Association of County Directors of Social Services.

The uncertainty around what welfare reform would mean, says Hirsch, was quickly replaced by something close to shock at the huge number of cases that simply dropped off the rolls as soon as the work requirements kicked in. And the drop not only proved to be permanent but continued to ratchet down.

The transformation has been profound, and that is why Hirsch says the county and state have substantially moved out of the cash-assistance game. "Welfare isn't a cash-assistance check anymore," she says, "But that doesn't mean we're not giving people help." What has shifted, she says, is the nature of the county's social services caseload: from those on traditional welfare to working poor who "struggle with food, health care, child care."

Other jurisdictions report a similar shift. "No one really even talks about welfare anymore because the caseload numbers have gone down so much," says Suzanne Wagner, a research assistant with Project Match, a welfare-to-work organization. "TANF is no longer seen as an avenue for intervention."

Which may be the shape of the new welfare reality, say seasoned veterans, such as New York's David Hansell: Even as TANF replaced the old welfare system,

TANF itself is being supplanted by a network of other types of assistance programs aimed at helping the working poor stay employed or simply survive once they are off the TANF rolls. "Most of the people who leave TANF leave for low-wage jobs that don't bring them close to the poverty level," Hansell says. "So now we're thinking about what is our responsibility after people leave public assistance and how can we support them economically."

Unfinished Business[*]

By Thomas Massaro
Commonweal, February 29, 2008

What ever happened to welfare reform? Our nation's financial assistance to low-income (and usually single-parent) families was a hot-button issue in the 1990s, but since then it seems to have vanished from our collective radar. In the debates among presidential candidates of both parties, welfare reform has been obscured by other issues. Until the recent economic downturn, post-9/11 concerns about security, terrorism, immigration, Iraq, and now Iran made it hard to pay adequate attention to domestic policy in general, and social-welfare policy in particular. Yet for the millions of Americans—most of them children—whose lives are directly affected by even the slightest change in federal welfare regulations, the future of the welfare system is an important matter. While the positions staked out on this issue by candidates and their parties may appear as mere afterthoughts in this campaign season, it is a mistake for voters to think of welfare as a minor issue—or to imagine that welfare reform is finished business. Grinding poverty persists in our country, even if many of us fail to notice it.

Temporary Assistance for Needy Families (TANF) is our nation's major cash-assistance program for low-income families, having replaced Aid to Families with Dependent Children (AFDC) in 1996. TANF is small potatoes by most budgetary measures. Its $16.5 billion annual budget is tiny compared to our annual expenditures on the military ($16.5 billion would fund the Iraq occupation for a few weeks). TANF was designed to save federal money, and no one can deny that it has.

But the reformed program was also supposed to be good for the poor: it would be, we were told, both more efficient and more effective. Of course, the only way to verify its effectiveness is to study its results, but so far the federal government hasn't shown much interest in the results. Until it does, the welfare reform of the '90s will remain seriously incomplete. The Personal Responsibility and Work Opportunity Reconciliation Act, which was passed by Newt Gingrich's Republican-controlled Congress and signed into law by Bill Clinton in the summer of 1996, called for a thorough review and reauthorization after six years. Almost twelve years later, there has still been no real review and the program has been temporarily extended rather than reauthorized. Since politicians were convinced that the welfare problem had been solved, there seemed no need to make sure that it had been.

The period of 1996–2002 witnessed so many simultaneous innovations in federal welfare policy that even ardent supporters of reform acknowledged the need for a thorough review of its effects. Insofar as these have been measured, they defy even the most informed predictions. Nobody could have known in advance how the different features of the sweeping overhaul would interact with each other and with new demographic and economic trends. The reform included the block-granting to states of what had previously been a matching-grant entitlement, time limits on benefits, work requirements, and a reduction in federal oversight of local welfare administration. States also enjoyed new freedom to impose behavioral rules on welfare recipients. If the recipients broke these rules, they lost their eligibility. States could now adopt "family caps" and exclude teenage mothers. Such policies encourage abortion and impose hardships on particular groups of applicants and recipients. This is one reason the U.S. Catholic bishops have consistently expressed serious reservations about the welfare reforms of the '90s.

After many months of contentious debate, frustrated opponents and triumphant supporters of the 1996 law agreed on little except this: Over time, the law would surely require adjustments, corrections, fine-tuning, and revisions. Both Republicans and Democrats insisted that special vigilance would be required to insure that the reform stayed on track and responded to the many variables in play. Opponents of the law worried that vicissitudes of the business cycle and other unpredictable trends would do severe damage to the low-income families and communities most affected by the reform. Supporters emphasized the wisdom of using states as laboratories for policy change. The whole point of increasing state autonomy was—or was supposed to be—to test the states' different policy responses. That way states could learn from the best practices of other states.

So the idea was to study the effects of welfare reform carefully—to make sure the reforms were working, and to compare one kind of reform with others. But that has not happened. No new resources have been devoted to measuring the effects of the 1996 law; and although President George W. Bush and congressional leaders drew up competing plans for a reauthorization package, none passed by the September 2002 target date. Years of capitol gridlock followed. Meanwhile, the TANF system was extended in its original form by a series of stopgap funding measures, usually in three-month increments. Finally, in spring 2007 all parties agreed to put off definitive congressional action on changing the welfare system until 2010. In the meantime, the policy can be altered only at the margins by executive orders.

In some ways, maintaining the status quo is a reasonably good outcome of the reauthorization battles. At the very least, this compromise prevents President

Bush from winning approval for several changes he advocates, including more severe work requirements. It also blocks funding for his expensive and controversial marriage-promotion campaign. Much of the credit for resisting the worst of the Bush proposals should go to Senator Olympia Snowe (R-Me.) who was a swing vote on the Senate Finance Committee in 2003. Snowe insisted that Bush's plan to push even more single mothers into the workforce could not be undertaken without a huge increase in federal child-care subsidies. By standing her ground on this point, which other Republicans viewed as a deal-breaker, Snowe effectively scuttled the president's reauthorization package and prolonged the deadlock.

Much more could be said about the politics and ethics of the reauthorization saga, but the main problem then as now was the failure of lawmakers to review the effects of our welfare policies, including those that have been adopted by the states. Government officials must not shy away from addressing complex issues, such as the interaction of the TANF program with food stamps, Medicaid, the Earned Income Tax Credit, and other work-support programs. It's easy to forget that the 1996 welfare law was an experiment intended to last six years, not twelve or fourteen. Like any scientific experiment, social experiments have to be monitored and their results measured, especially when they concern the most vulnerable citizens in our country.

So how should we measure the effects of welfare reform? The default metric has been the decline in the national TANF caseload. While it's true that the number of families receiving benefits has declined by about 60 percent since 1996, this statistic in isolation does not tell us all we need to know. A comprehensive evaluation of TANF must inquire into what happens to families that have left the welfare rolls, voluntarily or otherwise. Only after we have measured how they are faring will we be able to say with any confidence that welfare reform has been a success. Studies of "welfare-leaver" families abound, but few government officials are paying adequate attention to the data that already exist, and still fewer have sponsored studies to gather new data.

What, then, may we hope for in the 2008 election? As a proponent of more generous social assistance to disadvantaged families, I hope for a reform of TANF. Anyone who cares about improving the welfare system will at least want the winning candidates for national office to be committed to a careful review of our current welfare policies. Are they willing to look beyond one-dimensional measures of success and consider the actual lives of the urban and rural poor? Are candidates interested enough in low-income families to push beyond a few reassuring statistics and consider the concrete burdens imposed by a welfare system that now relies almost exclusively on getting people to work rather than making sure they have enough income to feed themselves and their families, whether or not they have jobs? Will politicians spend any of the political capital they acquire in this year's election to demand that the whole country pay serious attention to the lives and prospects of those who are struggling to survive?

If we do pay attention, it will be partly because welfare is no longer quite so prone to the politics of scapegoating as it used to be. Welfare recipients were once demonized as feckless, improvident, and lazy. One positive result of turning the welfare poor into the working poor—as recent policy has been designed to do—is that it changes the political equation that made welfare an important wedge issue of the 1980s and '90s. Perhaps this country is finally ready to consider antipoverty policies on their merits, rather than debate the worthiness of the people these policies are designed to serve.

Our nation's recent tendency to be utterly distracted by security issues is understandable, but it is nevertheless regrettable. Both voters and policymakers must learn to practice that quintessential twenty-first-century skill, multitasking. Without forgetting about the other large problems we face, we must find a corner of our consciousness where we can attend to the real effects of welfare reform and the real problems the poor continue to face in our society of superabundance. It is perhaps not the most frightening problem our elected leaders will address, and it certainly is not the newest. But for millions of struggling Americans, the stakes could not be higher.

Welfare Aid Isn't Growing as Economy Drops Off[*]

By Jason DeParle

The New York Times, February 1, 2009

Despite soaring unemployment and the worst economic crisis in decades, 18 states cut their welfare rolls last year, and nationally the number of people receiving cash assistance remained at or near the lowest in more than 40 years.

The trends, based on an analysis of new state data collected by *The New York Times*, raise questions about how well a revamped welfare system with great state discretion is responding to growing hardships.

Michigan cut its welfare rolls 13 percent, though it was one of two states whose October unemployment rate topped 9 percent. Rhode Island, the other, had the nation's largest welfare decline, 17 percent.

Of the 12 states where joblessness grew most rapidly, eight reduced or kept constant the number of people receiving Temporary Assistance for Needy Families, the main cash welfare program for families with children. Nationally, for the 12 months ending October 2008, the rolls inched up a fraction of 1 percent.

The deepening recession offers a fresh challenge to the program, which was passed by a Republican Congress and signed by President Bill Clinton in 1996 amid bitter protest and became one of the most closely watched social experiments in modern memory.

The program, which mostly serves single mothers, ended a 60-year-old entitlement to cash aid, replacing it with time limits and work requirements, and giving states latitude to discourage people from joining the welfare rolls. While it was widely praised in the boom years that followed, skeptics warned it would fail the needy when times turned tough.

Supporters of the program say the flat caseloads may reflect a lag between the loss of a job and the decision to seek help. They also say the recession may have initially spared the low-skilled jobs that many poor people take.

But critics argue that years of pressure to cut the welfare rolls has left an obstacle-ridden program that chases off the poor, even when times are difficult.

Even some of the program's staunchest defenders are alarmed.

"There is ample reason to be concerned here," said Ron Haskins, a former Republican Congressional aide who helped write the 1996 law overhauling the welfare system. "The overall structure is not working the way it was designed to work. We would expect, just on the face it, that when a deep recession happens, people could go back on welfare."

"When we started this, Democratic and Republican governors alike said, 'We know what's best for our state; we're not going to let people starve,' " said Mr. Haskins, who is now a researcher at the Brookings Institution in Washington. "And now that the chips are down, and unemployment is going up, most states are not doing enough to help families get back on the rolls."

The program's structure—fixed federal financing, despite caseload size—may discourage states from helping more people because the states bear all of the increased costs. By contrast, the federal government pays virtually all food-stamp costs, and last year every state expanded its food-stamp rolls; nationally, the food program grew 12 percent.

The clashing trends in some states—more food stamps, but less cash aid—suggest a safety net at odds with itself. Georgia shrank the cash welfare rolls by nearly 11 percent and expanded food stamps by 17 percent. After years of pushing reductions, Congress is now considering a rare plan that would subsidize expansions of the cash welfare rolls. The economic stimulus bills pending in Congress would provide matching grants—estimated at $2.5 billion over two years—to states with caseload expansions.

Born from Mr. Clinton's pledge to "end welfare as we know it," the new program brought furious protests from people who predicted the poor would suffer. Then millions of people quickly left the rolls, employment rates rose and child poverty plunged.

But the economy of the late 1990s was unusually strong, and even then critics warned that officials placed too much stress on caseload reduction. With benefits harder to get, a small but growing share of families was left with neither welfare nor work and fell deeper into destitution.

"TANF is not an especially attractive option for most people," said Linda Blanchette, a top welfare official in Pennsylvania, which cut its rolls last year by 6 percent. "People really do view it as a last resort."

The data collected by *The Times* is the most recent available for every state and includes some similar programs financed solely by states, to give the broadest picture of cash aid. In a year when 1.1 million jobs disappeared, 18 states cut the rolls, 20 states expanded them, and caseloads in 12 states remained essentially flat, fluctuating less than 3 percent. (In addition, caseloads in the District of Columbia rose by nearly 5 percent.)

The rolls rose 7 percent in the West, stayed flat in the South, and fell in the Northeast by 4 percent and Midwest by 5 percent.

Seven states increased their rolls by double digits. Five states, including Texas and Michigan, made double-digit reductions. Of the 10 states with the highest child poverty rates, eight kept caseloads level or further reduced the rolls.

"This is evidence of a strikingly unresponsive system," said Mark H. Greenberg, co-director of a poverty institute at the Georgetown University law school. Some administrators disagree.

"We're still putting people to work," said Larry Temple, who runs the job placement program for welfare recipients in Texas, where the rolls dropped 15 percent. "A lot of the occupations that historically we've been able to put the welfare people in are still hiring. Home health is a big one."

Though some welfare recipients continue to find jobs, nationally their prospects have worsened. Joblessness among women ages 20 to 24 without a high school degree rose to 23.9 percent last year, from 17.9 percent the year before, according to the Bureau of Labor Statistics.

Some analysts offer a different reason for the Texas caseload declines: a policy that quickly halts all cash aid to recipients who fail to attend work programs.

"We're really just pushing families off the program," said Celia Hagert of the Center for Public Policy Priorities, a research and advocacy group in Austin, Tex.

Some officials predict the rolls will yet rise. "There's typically a one- to two-year lag between an economic downturn and an uptick in the welfare rolls," said David Hansell, who oversees the program in New York State, where the rolls fell 4 percent.

Indeed, as the recession has worsened in recent months, some states' rolls have just started to grow. Georgia's caseload fell until July 2008, but has since risen 5 percent. Still, as of October the national caseloads remained down 70 percent from their peak in the early 1990s under the predecessor program, Aid to Families with Dependent Children.

Nationally, caseloads fell every year from 1994 to 2007, to about 4.1 million people, a level last seen in 1964. The federal total for 2008 has not been published, but the *Times* analysis of state data suggests they remained essentially flat.

Some recent caseload reduction has been driven by a 2006 law that required states to place more recipients in work programs, which can be costly and difficult to run. It threatened states with stiff fines but eased the targets for states that simply cut the rolls.

"Some states decided they had to get tougher," said Sharon Parrott of the Center for Budget and Policy Priorities, a Washington research and advocacy group.

Rhode Island was among them. Previously, the state had reduced but not eliminated grants to families in which an adult had hit a 60-month limit. Last year, it closed those cases, removing 2,200 children from the rolls.

Under the new federal accounting rules, that made it easier to meet statistical goals and protected the state from fines.

Michigan also imposed new restrictions, forcing applicants to spend a month in a job-search program before collecting benefits. Critics say the up-front requirement poses obstacles to the neediest applicants, like those with physical or mental illnesses.

"I think that's a legitimate complaint," said Ismael Ahmed, director of the Michigan Department of Human Services, though he blamed the federal rules. The program "was drawn for an economy that is not the economy most states are in."

While food stamps usually grow faster than cash aid during recessions, the current contrast is stark. Many officials see cash aid in a negative light, as a form of dependency, while encouraging the use of food stamps and calling them nutritional support.

"Food assistance is not considered welfare," said Donalda Carlson, a Rhode Island welfare administrator.

Nationally, the temporary assistance program gives states $16.8 billion a year—the same amount they received in the early 1990s, when caseloads were more than three times as high as they are now. Mr. Haskins, the program's architect, said that obliged them to ensure the needy could return to the rolls. "States have plenty of money," he said.

But most states have shifted the money into other programs—including child care and child welfare—and say they cannot shift it back without causing other problems.

Oregon expanded its cash caseload 19 percent last year, so far without major backlash. "That's the purpose of the program—to be there for that need," said Vic Todd, a senior state official. But California officials expressed ambivalence about a 6 percent rise in the cash welfare rolls in that state when it is facing a $40 billion deficit. "There's some fine tuning of the program that needs to occur, to incentivize work," said John Wagner, the state director of social services.

Among those sanguine about current caseload trends is Robert Rector, an analyst at the Heritage Foundation in Washington who is influential with conservative policy makers. He said the program had "reduced poverty beyond anyone's expectations" and efforts to dilute its rigor would only harm the poor.

"We need to continue with the principle that you give assistance willingly, but you require the individual to prepare for self-sufficiency," he said.

3

The Medicaid and SCHIP Debates

Editor's Introduction

In 2008 about 46 million Americans, including 9 million children, lacked access to health insurance. Although there is virtually universal agreement that health care in the United States is in dire need of reform, policymakers do not agree on what should be done about it. In recent years, as a result of a downwardly spiraling global economy, the two government health insurance programs aimed at serving low-income Americans, Medicaid and State Children's Health Insurance Program (SCHIP), have been stretched to cover an ever-increasing portion of the population. In lieu of what will inevitably need to take place—an overhaul of the nation's health-care system—heated partisan debates have raged in Congress over how to reform Medicaid and SCHIP so that they can better meet the country's seemingly endless demand for low-cost health insurance.

For generations, the U.S. health-care system has centered on employer-provided health insurance, a structure that inevitably leaves out millions of Americans who lack access to insurance through their employers and cannot afford to purchase health insurance on their own. Cracks in the system have widened in recent years as ballooning health-care costs have lead insurance companies to charge higher premiums and employers to cover fewer costs or drop insurance plans altogether. To help fill in these cracks, since 1965, the government has provided health insurance to several groups of low-income Americans—including parents, children, seniors, and people with disabilities—through the Medicaid program. Funded by the federal government through grants tailored to each state's poverty level, Medicaid programs are designed and implemented by the states within the framework established by the federal government. Medicaid became a popular and important program—particularly for children and the elderly—and over the years a number of reforms were instituted to expand its reach.

In 1997 Congress passed the State Children's Health Insurance Program (SCHIP) in an effort to insure children who still fell into the system's cracks, such as those belonging to families that earned too much money to qualify for Medicaid but not enough to purchase independent health insurance. Like Medicaid, SCHIP was designed as a jointly financed federal and state program. It allowed states a high degree of flexibility within the broad federal guidelines that mandated coverage to children and families with incomes up to 200 percent of the federal poverty level. By 1999 all 50 states and each of the territories had approved SCHIP plans. Over ten years, the federal government provided $40 billion to states through SCHIP, and the program was credited with insuring more than 5 million children across the country.

Over time, however, both Medicaid and SCHIP faced familiar problems: rising costs, funding shortfalls, and apparent inefficiency. Criticisms arose from both sides of the political aisle. Republicans decried Medicaid for being costly and inefficient and argued that it discouraged recipients from seeking private health plans. They called for easing federal regulation of the program so that states could introduce cost-sharing measures, such as patient co-payments, to help shoulder the burden of coverage. Such arguments formed the basis of the Medicaid reforms contained in the Deficit Reduction Act of 2005, signed into law by President George W. Bush, which had far-reaching cost-cutting effects on a wide array of social programs. The new regulations gave states greater authority to shift the cost burden away from the government through a variety of measures, including directing enrollees to private "benchmark" managed-care plans. One of the most significant and controversial reforms was the requirement that eligible applicants provide proof of citizenship—as opposed to simple verbal affirmation, under the old system—when they apply for Medicaid, a provision that many argued would lead to discrimination against underprivileged populations.

Meanwhile, to cover the growing numbers of uninsured Americans, a bipartisan group in Congress began calling for an expansion of the SCHIP program for the millions of children and families who did not qualify for either Medicaid or SCHIP, but still struggled to purchase adequate health insurance. In his two terms in office, President Bush vetoed two bipartisan bills aimed at expanding the SCHIP program to cover 4 million uninsured children, paid for with $35 billion raised through a tobacco tax increase. Bush and other Republicans argued that the proposed expansion would change the original intent of the program—to provide insurance for the poor—by expanding it to cover some middle-class children who were already covered by private plans. In December 2007, Bush reauthorized SCHIP at its current funding levels. Just over one year later, however, President Barack Obama effectively settled the debate by signing into law legislation that expanded SCHIP to an additional 4 million children, using $33 billion raised over four and a half years.

The selections contained in this section offer a variety of perspectives on the recent debates surrounding Medicaid and SCHIP. In the first article, "Reforming Medicaid," John C. Goodman and Devon M. Herrick outline the immense costs and inefficiencies of Medicaid and present their case for why the program should adopt cost-sharing and market-based reforms. Gary Enos addresses a similar topic in the second selection, "Something of Value," but argues that cost-sharing measures will not necessarily instill personal responsibility in all groups of Medicaid beneficiaries and, in fact, are likely to cause hardship for certain populations. In "SCHIP and Beyond," Jonathan Walters contends that the cost-sharing elements of an expanded SCHIP could be used as a model for a future universal health insurance plan. The following two articles, "An Immoral Philosophy," by Nobel Prize-winning economist and *New York Times* columnist Paul Krugman, and "Sleepwalking Toward DD-Day," by the Pulitzer-Prize winning conservative journalist George F. Will, offer contrasting and impassioned perspectives on SCHIP expansion.

The final article, by Jennifer Lubell for *Modern Healthcare,* outlines what was accomplished with Obama's recent SCHIP-expansion bill and what still needs to be defined.

Reforming Medicaid[*]

By John C. Goodman and Devon M. Herrick
USA Today, September 2005

Medicaid is the largest single expenditure state governments face today. The
country as a whole spends more on Medicaid than on primary and secondary
education. We also spend more on Medicaid (for the poor) than on Medicare (for
the elderly)—and at the rate the program is growing, it is on a course to consume
the entire budgets of state governments in just a few decades.

The Bush Administration's budget proposes to reduce projected spending by
$10,000,000,000 over the next five years, and some members of Congress want
a commission to recommend additional reforms. The nation's governors are preparing their own proposal.

Medicaid is a complex system of Federal matching funds with special pots of
money limited to specific uses. This often results in wasteful spending. Currently,
states are required to cover certain populations, such as the disabled and pregnant mothers. States can receive additional matching funds to cover other seg-
ments as well—for example, children in families who earn too much to qualify
for Medicaid. Although coverage for some services is mandated, others, including
prescription drugs, are optional. Yet, about two-thirds of Medicaid spending is on
optional populations and benefits.

The biggest problem is that, for every 40 cents spent by the states, the Federal
government chips in 60 cents. Thus, states are tempted to go for the matching
funds even when they know the spending is wasteful. The matching scheme also
is a bad deal for taxpayers. The average cost per Medicaid beneficiary nationwide
is about $7,500. However, since New York offers almost all optional benefits to
all optional enrollees, it spends almost double the national average. Mississippi,
which has a less generous benefit package and confines coverage mostly to the
"mandatory" poor, spends just about half the national average. The result is that
New York receives about twice as much Federal money per enrollee as Mississippi,
where the need is much greater.

The practice of matching grants coupled with wasteful regulations has to end. States instead should request block grants covering all Medicaid costs, State Children's Health Insurance Program expenses, and disproportionate share hospital funds. States should have complete discretion, provided they spend the funds on indigent care.

Private health plans are a much more efficient way to provide care than traditional Medicaid. Yet, Federal payment schemes can discourage their use. For example, Texas has announced plans to place 2,800,000 urban Medicaid recipients into managed care health plans at an estimated savings of $109,000,000 over two years. However, the proposal is being opposed by public hospitals that stand to lose $75,000,000 worth of Federally-funded disproportionate share payments relating to indigent care.

Medicaid is an alternative to private insurance, and when the public sector expands, the private sector contracts. After all, why pay for insurance when it is available for free? Studies show that, for every extra one dollar spent on Medicaid, spending on private insurance contracts by 50–75 cents. During the 1990s, for instance, despite a large expansion in Medicaid spending, the uninsured rate went up, not down. That process must be reversed. States need to use Medicaid funds to enroll beneficiaries in private insurance—individually-owned and employer-provided. There are enormous potential savings if, for example, the state could pay the employee's portion of employer-provided insurance premiums, letting the employer pay the bulk of the costs. Current regulations, however, make this reform difficult, if not impossible.

Health savings accounts would help as well. Studies show that patients with diabetes, asthma, heart disease, and other chronic conditions can reduce costs and improve quality by managing their own care. Yet, self-managed care will be successful only if patients also manage some of their own health care dollars.

At least 25 states are experimenting with Cash and Counsel programs that allow disabled patients to manage their own money. Bureaucratic rules, however, work mostly in the opposite direction. For instance, Medicaid regulations limit cost-sharing by patients to nominal amounts, and forbid it outright for selected populations. States that have copayments are allowed to charge enrollees only three dollars or less for prescription drugs.

Nearly half of Medicaid spending is for long-term care. Nationally, more than two-thirds of nursing home costs are paid for by Medicaid—about double the rate a decade ago. Legal loopholes allow individuals to meet Medicaid's asset test by transferring money and property to offspring prior to entering a nursing home. Many couples have disguised what they own by divorcing, assigning joint property to the "well spouse" while the "ill spouse" receives none. An entire "elder law" industry has sprung up in recent years to assist the elderly in hiding assets so Medicaid will cover their long-term care costs.

In response, states need to give seniors financial incentives to choose home care over residential care and residential managed care over nursing home care. A pilot project in four states called the Partnerships for Long Term Care (PLTC) provides financial incentives to purchase long-term care insurance. The plan allows consumers to shelter their assets by purchasing a qualifying private insurance policy with a defined amount of coverage. When policyholders enter a nursing home, they first rely on the insurance. When they have exhausted their insurance, special eligibility rules allow them to receive Medicaid benefits while retaining assets equal to the value of the policy. For instance, a long-term care policy with $120,000 in benefits allows an individual to shelter $120,000 in assets and still qualify for Medicaid long-term care. Since the average nursing home stay is a little more than one year, very few of those who have purchased policies have had to apply for Medicaid benefits. An inflexible 1993 Federal law effectively limited PLTC to the four states that already had pilot projects. Repeal of the law would allow other states to establish similar programs.

Something of Value[*]

By Gary Enos
Governing, January 2006

Medicaid has long been wary of asking beneficiaries to share the costs of their care. For most recipients, the program has not permitted premiums or anything beyond very minimal co-payments for a limited number of services. But that's likely to change—and soon. Medicaid officials at both the state and federal levels argue that the free ride is as outmoded in medicine as the house call.

For a model on cost sharing, many are looking at the State Children's Health Insurance Program (SCHIP), which covers young people with somewhat higher family incomes than those who receive traditional Medicaid benefits. There, states have more leeway to impose charges and participants with incomes above 150 percent of the federal poverty line can be asked to pay a cost-share of up to 5 percent of family income. The preliminary report on Medicaid reform from the National Governors Association (NGA) calls for Medicaid to follow SCHIP and to allow cost sharing but with a 5 percent cap for all beneficiaries, which the NGA considered "a critical balance to this proposal."

That's not the only cost-sharing suggestion out there. The federal Medicaid Commission would like to give states flexibility to increase co-payments on non-preferred drugs above the current nominal maximum of $3 per prescription—to enourage "cost-effective utilization." The Centers for Medicare & Medicaid Services estimates that $2 billion could be saved over the next five years if states were allowed to increase their caps in a variety of ways.

Out in the states, these proposals find sympathetic ears. Many state officials—Medicaid directors among them—deem co-payments, deductibles and premiums entirely appropriate in a time when nearly all Americans are expected to pay something for each physician visit or prescription. They argue that a lack of financial accountability encourages beneficiaries to use medical care when it's not necessary.

"You have to have some economic tension—people have to have some skin in the game," says Tennessee Governor Phil Bredesen. He adds that it's not enough to dismiss co-payments on the basis of poverty since most other services ask for some payment by the poor. "At faith-based clinics," he points out, "they take it as an article of faith that everyone has to pay something for the service—that what you get for free, you don't value."

Bredesen's argument appeals to the American ideal of self-sufficiency, and it is a cornerstone of the NGA report. "The purpose of increased cost-sharing is not to restrict access to necessary medical care," it states, "but to allow individuals to contribute to the costs of their own health care as much as possible. These new policies would be monitored and evaluated heavily, and if the evidence shows that increased cost sharing harms appropriate access, the policies should be revised."

CHECK OUT THE EVIDENCE

Currently, most state officials have difficulty producing hard data to prove claims that this technique will instill personal responsibility in Medicaid beneficiaries and thus save money. In fact, some observers argue that co-payments, deductibles and similar requirements may result in clients' failing to access services or dropping coverage altogether. Preventive care, which can easily be delayed or ignored, may well be the first casualty. This ultimately can endanger the health of medically needy citizens and eventually generate higher costs in the system.

Washington State's governor, Christine Gregoire, is particularly concerned about preventive care and has emphasized the importance of getting coverage for all the eligible children in her state. So, when Washington received federal approval to impose a $10 monthly premium for families at 150 to 200 percent of poverty, she suspended that particular plan.

One factor that makes the debate over cost sharing so complicated is that the Medicaid population is not homogeneous. According to Chuck Duarte, administrator of the Nevada Division of Health Care Financing and Policy, co-payments and other charges work "for higher-income populations, who are more used to insurance products that use cost sharing. But for the aged and disabled population, with multiple prescriptions and frequent physician services, cost sharing is not going to be an effective tool. These people already have a hard time paying for whatever they have to pay for to stay alive."

A few years ago, Vermont imposed premiums on higher-income groups in its Medicaid and SCHIP programs. Forty thousand people were hit with the premiums in December 2003. The following month, 11 percent of those clients were disenrolled for nonpayment of premiums. However, just a month later, about one-third of the disenrolled paid their way back into the program. Vermont officials say they generally have seen this pattern when they increase cost-sharing requirements.

Joshua Slen, director of Medicaid in Vermont, is not alarmed about the drop-off in Medicaid rolls. Slen—and a number of others—believe that those who stay out of Medicaid after premiums are increased are a generally healthier group than those who stay in the program. "If you look at the program," he says, "it's clear that the people with higher levels of need continue to pay the premium."

THE OREGON CASE

Medicaid-eligibles in the entitlement portion of the Oregon Health Plan are not required to pay premiums or co-payments. But a federal waiver in early 2003 allowed the state to tighten up on other Medicaid beneficiaries. This group falls under the Oregon Health Plan Standard (OHP Standard) portion of the Medicaid program where state officials increased the premiums to a range of $6 to $20 a month based on income and also tightened rules on nonpayment. They lifted exemptions from the premiums for such "hardship" groups as the homeless and imposed stricter payment deadlines that, if unmet, resulted in an immediate loss of Medicaid eligibility for six months. In addition, many adults covered under OHP Standard were subject to co-payments of $3 to $250 for most covered services.

Shortly after these changes were imposed, enrollment in OHP Standard dropped significantly—from 95,000 in February 2003 to just over 50,000 by the end of the year. At the lowest income level, 59 percent of beneficiaries with no incomes lost their Medicaid coverage after being required to pay a $6 monthly premium.

"While it is difficult to do a cause-and-effect because so many other changes were going on at the time, this was the most salient factor in the decline in program enrollment," says Lynn Read, acting administrator of the Oregon Office of Medical Assistance Programs. "It's clear that there were significant hardships as a result of premiums."

An analysis by the Kaiser Commission on Medicaid and the Uninsured found that 72 percent of those who had been disenrolled from Medicaid had remained uninsured. Only 11 percent returned to OHP, and even fewer found employer-sponsored coverage.

The analysis also noted that physicians in the Portland area reported that patients were "self-selecting not to schedule follow-up visits, and, as a result, their health outcomes are getting progressively worse." One Medicaid participant said she raised money for her co-payments by buying small bags of potato chips with food stamps and then selling them for cash in office areas of her community at lunchtime.

Advocates in Oregon sued the state and the federal government over the mandatory premiums and co-payments, saying CMS did not have the authority to waive statutory restrictions on cost sharing. The state government prevailed on the premiums issue but not on co-payments. It has not enforced co-payments under OHP Standard since June 2004.

Some states have since held off on plans to seek waiver approval for stricter cost-sharing requirements, and several state health care officials have expressed their doubts about its effectiveness, particularly for the most financially vulnerable. "There may be some argument for selective co-payments, in areas such as inappropriate ER utilization, says Mark Moody, administrator of the Wisconsin Division of Health Care Financing. "But seeking 'flexibility' in this area is often code for 'flexibility to cut benefits.'"

SCHIP and Beyond[*]

By Jonathan Walters
Governing, March 2007

Delivering health care to the uninsured hasn't been a very visible issue in Congress since the failure of Hillary Clinton's massive and cumbersome reform scheme in 1994. But it's about to come back. The first real test of political sentiment will be the upcoming debate on reauthorization of the State Children's Health Insurance Program, SCHIP, which was created in 1997 as a 10-year, $40 billion partnership between states and the federal government. SCHIP extends coverage to children whose families aren't poor enough for Medicaid but still can't afford to buy private coverage.

Under SCHIP, the states and the federal government share the cost of coverage, but states are accorded considerable flexibility in creating their own plans. And so 50 states and the District of Columbia have been largely free to experiment with ways to develop healthy kids, while trying to figure out how to keep costs as low as possible.

The cost issue has been particularly important with SCHIP inasmuch as the program is not fiscally open-ended. Unlike Medicaid, SCHIP is a straight grant program, with finite amounts of federal money flowing to states. And so state health agencies have had to be very mindful of costs as they seek to expand coverage.

Although limited in scope, the program has been credited with extending health care to more than 5 million children all over the country. And while detailed studies on the positive health consequences of that coverage are perplexingly hard to come by, no one seriously disputes that setting kids on a healthier path early in life pays dividends.

As Congress begins to debate reauthorization of SCHIP, a couple of points are important to keep in mind, one about the program itself, and the other about what SCHIP tells us with regard to the broader issue of health care coverage for the more than 40 million Americans of all ages who do not have it now.

SCHIP needs an infusion of additional money if it is to reach the universe of eligible kids that program advocates have always wanted to reach. In fact, though, SCHIP needs more money just to tread water. If the program were to be reauthorized at current levels, analysts estimate that the rising cost of health care would require that more than a quarter of the children currently covered by the program be dropped.

But beyond the issue of funding, SCHIP needs reauthorization and replenishment because it represents a first step toward the kind of larger program that an increasing number of experts now see as inevitable.

The most fundamental lesson that SCHIP has to teach is that a strong partnership between states and the federal government can be the foundation on which to base expanded health care coverage. It is a model that embraces state experimentation along with federal support, and not just fiscal support but also analytical support aimed at finding successful programs.

The state-federal partnership angle is equally important from the standpoint of pragmatic politics. A federally enacted health care plan that allows for a wide variety of state-designed and implemented coverage experiments, and can be phased in to existence in cooperation with all relevant statewide interest groups, has a much better chance of political survival than any giant federally based monolith, or yet another set of complicated changes to our tax code aimed at altering markets and human behavior.

In other words, there's a potentially attractive middle ground between universal coverage and tax-code tinkering, and that middle ground lies in some sort of cost-sharing formula between the feds and states along the lines of SCHIP. States would be given some money and then cut loose to experiment with ways of extending coverage beyond children.

Discussion of that scenario should go forward independent of SCHIP reauthorization. SCHIP may be a model—and perhaps even a platform—for wider coverage, but for now, states and the federal government should be working hard to preserve and strengthen the existing program. Then they need to turn to a serious examination of the lessons the program might offer when it comes to broadening coverage to more Americans.

An Immoral Philosophy[*]

By Paul Krugman
The New York Times, July 30, 2007

When a child is enrolled in the State Children's Health Insurance Program (Schip), the positive results can be dramatic. For example, after asthmatic children are enrolled in Schip, the frequency of their attacks declines on average by 60 percent, and their likelihood of being hospitalized for the condition declines more than 70 percent.

Regular care, in other words, makes a big difference. That's why Congressional Democrats, with support from many Republicans, are trying to expand Schip, which already provides essential medical care to millions of children, to cover millions of additional children who would otherwise lack health insurance.

But President Bush says that access to care is no problem—"After all, you just go to an emergency room"—and, with the support of the Republican Congressional leadership, he's declared that he'll veto any Schip expansion on "philosophical" grounds.

It must be about philosophy, because it surely isn't about cost. One of the plans Mr. Bush opposes, the one approved by an overwhelming bipartisan majority in the Senate Finance Committee, would cost less over the next five years than we'll spend in Iraq in the next four months. And it would be fully paid for by an increase in tobacco taxes.

The House plan, which would cover more children, is more expensive, but it offsets Schip costs by reducing subsidies to Medicare Advantage—a privatization scheme that pays insurance companies to provide coverage, and costs taxpayers 12 percent more per beneficiary than traditional Medicare.

Strange to say, however, the administration, although determined to prevent any expansion of children's health care, is also dead set against any cut in Medicare Advantage payments.

So what kind of philosophy says that it's O.K. to subsidize insurance companies, but not to provide health care to children?

Well, here's what Mr. Bush said after explaining that emergency rooms provide all the health care you need: "They're going to increase the number of folks eligible through Schip; some want to lower the age for Medicare. And then all of a sudden, you begin to see a—I wouldn't call it a plot, just a strategy—to get more people to be a part of a federalization of health care."

Now, why should Mr. Bush fear that insuring uninsured children would lead to a further "federalization" of health care, even though nothing like that is actually in either the Senate plan or the House plan? It's not because he thinks the plans wouldn't work. It's because he's afraid that they would. That is, he fears that voters, having seen how the government can help children, would ask why it can't do the same for adults.

And there you have the core of Mr. Bush's philosophy. He wants the public to believe that government is always the problem, never the solution. But it's hard to convince people that government is always bad when they see it doing good things. So his philosophy says that the government must be prevented from solving problems, even if it can. In fact, the more good a proposed government program would do, the more fiercely it must be opposed.

This sounds like a caricature, but it isn't. The truth is that this good-is-bad philosophy has always been at the core of Republican opposition to health care reform. Thus back in 1994, William Kristol warned against passage of the Clinton health care plan "in any form," because "its success would signal the rebirth of centralized welfare-state policy at the very moment that such policy is being perceived as a failure in other areas."

But it has taken the fight over children's health insurance to bring the perversity of this philosophy fully into view.

There are arguments you can make against programs, like Social Security, that provide a safety net for adults. I can respect those arguments, even though I disagree. But denying basic health care to children whose parents lack the means to pay for it, simply because you're afraid that success in insuring children might put big government in a good light, is just morally wrong.

And the public understands that. According to a recent Georgetown University poll, 9 in 10 Americans—including 83 percent of self-identified Republicans—support an expansion of the children's health insurance program.

There is, it seems, more basic decency in the hearts of Americans than is dreamt of in Mr. Bush's philosophy.

Sleepwalking Toward DD-Day [*]

By George F. Will
Newsweek, October 8, 2007

Last Thursday was 96 days before DD-day, the day the Demographic Deluge begins. That is Jan. 1, when the first of 78 million baby boomers reach 62, the age at which a majority of Social Security recipients begin to receive that entitlement. Social Security is unsustainable as currently configured, but is a picture of health compared with another middle-class entitlement, Medicare.

On Thursday, the Senate, following the House, voted to create another open-ended middle-class entitlement—Congress is not inhibited by the Law of Holes, which is: When you are in a hole, quit digging.

Although it is the elderly who are devouring the federal budget—and through it, a huge share of the economy's future production—the State Children's Health Insurance Program is (mostly) about children, at least ostensibly. But it also is about a deep divide between the parties.

The struggle over SCHIP is an unusual Washington dust-up—one that actually is as portentous as Washingtonians, with their flair for (self)dramatization, say it is. It is a proxy fight over the future of the welfare state, meaning the trajectory of government and the burdens it will place on the economy, which, by its dynamism, must generate the revenues to pay the bills.

SCHIP was created in 1997 by a Republican-controlled Congress. Today's Democratic-controlled Congress wants to transform its mission. It began as a program whereby the federal government would subsidize state governments in providing health insurance for children from households not poor enough (generally 200 percent above the poverty line) to qualify for Medicaid but not affluent enough to afford to buy insurance. Were it to become law, the new SCHIP would be a long stride toward unlimited federal funds working as incentives for states to expand eligibility to more and more affluent families.

It would immediately include some with incomes 400 percent of the poverty line ($83,000 for a family of four). Over time, its "mission creep" would continue. Mike Leavitt, secretary of Health and Human Services, says that the new SCHIP would enroll 2.8 million more children, but 1.1 million of them would be from families for whom SCHIP had become an incentive to drop their private insurance. To that, some liberals say, sotto voce: Good.

Why? In the perennial tension between the competing values of freedom and equality, conservatives favor freedom, which inevitably increases unequal social outcomes. Liberals' mission is the promotion of equality, understood as equal dependence of more and more people for more and more things on government. Liberals increasingly define the public good in terms of the multiplication of entitlements. Conservatives increasingly understand their mission as the promotion of attitudes and aptitudes they think are weakened by that multiplication.

The president proposed a $5 billion increase for SCHIP over five years. In a familiar Washington folk dance, the Senate voted a $35 billion increase, and the House endorsed a $50 billion increase but receded to the Senate sum, which was therefore declared moderate. The increase supposedly would be funded by a 61-cent increase in the cigarette tax.

So, this health legislation depends on a constantly large and renewable supply of smokers—22 million new ones. This "progressive" measure requires a regressive tax (smokers are predominantly and increasingly lower class) levied to expand subsidized health insurance ever upward into the middle class.

The president proposes a plan to give everyone personal ownership of fully portable (not tied to employment) health insurance policies—tax deductions of $7,500 for individuals and $15,000 for families purchasing policies. Liberals complain that this would be an incentive for employers to stop providing coverage. To which conservatives respond: Good.

They say: If we can disentangle health care from the wage system, General Motors can go back to being a car and truck company rather than a health-care provider unsuccessfully struggling to sell cars and trucks fast enough to pay employees' and retirees' medical expenses. Some liberals want to preserve the entanglement until business clamors for government to nationalize the one seventh of the economy that is health care.

For philosophic reasons, Democrats wish the bill would become law. For political reasons, they welcome the president's promised veto, which will preserve for them the issue of Republican beastliness toward "the children."

It has become a verbal tic for politicians to say that everything they do is "about the children." This rhetoric of pathos reflects the de-intellectualization of public life—the substitution of sentimentalism for reasoned persuasion. Bill Clinton carried this to comic lengths when, in his first State of the Union address, he noted that "not a single Russian missile is pointed at the children of America."

Those children-seeking missiles were diabolical. The new SCHIP, which would expand the dependency of middle-class children on government, is not diabolical, but neither is it just "about the children."

Boost for SCHIP[*]

By Jennifer Lubell
Modern Healthcare, February 2009

Hospitals and other healthcare providers are banking on treating fewer children in the emergency department and providing more preventive services as a result of the extension and expansion of the State Children's Health Insurance Program signed into law last week.

The law expands SCHIP to cover an additional 4 million children on top of the 7 million it already covers, and it is expected to cost nearly $33 billion over 4½ years. For fiscal 2008 that figure was about $30 billion.

Moreover, shortly after President Barack Obama signed the bill into law, he rescinded an HHS policy that restricted the number of children that are allowed into the program, which is likely to lead to increased coverage of children.

The law also establishes a Medicaid and CHIP Payment and Access Commission to review and assess payment policies under Medicaid and the children's insurance program, and make recommendations to Congress on improvements in access to care under the programs.

The law doesn't include a provision in the House version that would have banned physician self-referral to hospitals in which they have an ownership interest.

Various healthcare advocacy and trade groups chimed in on their support of the SCHIP expansion. "Congress and the administration rightly recognize that, like education, healthcare is a basic prerequisite for kids to have a productive future. America's hospitals strongly support the reauthorization of SCHIP," said American Hospital Association President and Chief Executive Officer Richard Umbdenstock.

Hospitals in particular are taking Obama's statement that "no one should be receiving his care in the emergency room in the middle of the night" to heart.

"We currently have a significant percentage of emergency visits which are pediatric," said Thomas Brown, senior vice president with Nanticoke Health Services, Seaford, Del. "Many of these could have been seen in an outpatient setting. It is reasonable to conclude that lack of insurance has driven many of these visits to the emergency room."

Jim Mandell, CEO of 359-bed Children's Hospital, Boston, said he is hoping the number of uninsured children in Massachusetts "will get down to zero," now that the new SCHIP statute is in effect. Coupled with the state's universal coverage plan, it's a goal to reach for, he said.

Mandell specifically praised measures in the bill to simplify enrollment, and to develop quality measures for pediatrics. Such measures currently apply to Medicare, "but it's never been done for kids."

Developing measures across common areas of diseases and treatments for all providers in the country "should make a tremendous difference in improving quality of care," Mandell said.

Obama, in signing the new bill into law so expediently, plus quashing the controversial HHS policy that restricted SCHIP enrollment, indicated he was adamant about giving more children access to health insurance.

The policy, first issued on Aug. 17, 2007, required states to first enroll 95% of children in families earning less than 200% of the federal poverty level—$42,400 for a family of four—before they could enroll children in families earning more than 250% of the federal poverty level.

If the directive hadn't been withdrawn, more children would have been denied coverage, the president said in a memorandum to HHS. The directive was a "hotly debated issue, so it was a very important decision President Obama made to rescind these policies," said Molly Collins Offner, director for policy with the AHA.

Less clear is how many additional children will get SCHIP coverage, now that the HHS policy, for all intents and purposes, has been rescinded. The memo, in conjunction with the new SCHIP reauthorization bill, "opens doors to states to move forward with expansions that they hadn't acted on before, as well as new expansions to the program," said Judy Solomon, senior fellow with the Center on Budget and Policy Priorities.

4

Feeding America's Hungry:
Food Stamps/Supplemental Nutrition
Assistance Program

Editor's Introduction

Though outright starvation is rare in the United States, chronic under-nutrition continues to be a problem in certain impoverished sectors of society. A lack of regular nutritious meals has a profound effect on learning, concentration, productivity, and both physical and psychological health, especially among children. Despite the many anti-hunger programs that exist in the United States, over 35 million people are today classified as "food insecure," a category that includes those at risk of experiencing hunger. The Food Stamp Program, and other food assistance initiatives, have undergone reforms to change their focus—both expanding and contracting their coverage under various administrations. Many conservatives see the Food Stamp Program (whose name was changed in October 2008 to the Supplemental Nutrition Assistance Program, or SNAP) as one costly element of a larger welfare system that promotes inactivity and should be closely regulated, while many liberals and hunger advocates view freedom from hunger or "food insecurity" as a basic human right that should be an entitlement with few restrictions. Many have called on the government to expand the programs that make up a so-called "nutritional safety net," as well as to introduce reforms that might make food stamps unnecessary, such as establishing a living minimum wage and universal health care.

By far the nation's largest food assistance program, SNAP provides a means for those with little or no income to obtain a nutritionally adequate diet. Administered through the U.S. Department of Agriculture (USDA) Food and Nutrition Service, the Food Stamp Program was made permanent in 1964 by President Lyndon Johnson, as part of his "War on Poverty." It is an entitlement program whose recipients are determined by household size, income, assets, and other factors. The program's original aim was to address two problems: hungry low-income families and excess domestic agricultural products. As of 2004 the Food Stamp Program served about 24 million Americans at a cost of approximately $27 billion.

The program has undergone a number of changes since its inception. The first Food Stamp Act operated in 22 states and required participants to purchase low-cost food stamp coupons. In 1971 national eligibility standards were established by President Richard Nixon, and free food stamps were now distributed to the poorest citizens. By 1973 the program was a mandated entitlement in all 50 states. The Food Stamp Program expanded dramatically in 1977, when President Jimmy Carter eliminated the purchase requirement. Recipients no longer had to buy their food coupons; rather they received only the "bonus portion" of their coupon allotments, a change that led to a 3.5 million increase in enrollment.

In the 1980s and 1990s the Food Stamp Program, along with many other social-welfare initiatives, came under the scrutiny of administrations looking to cut government social spending. In light of record enrollment figures—in 1994 Food Stamp enrollment had reached 28 million—President Bill Clinton, as part of his Republican-supported reforms, instituted cuts to the Food Stamp Program as part of both the Personal Responsibility and Work Opportunities Reconciliation Act (PRWORA), in 1996, and the Balanced Budget Act, in 1997. One of the most controversial of the new regulations contained in PRWORA eliminated eligibility for almost all groups of legal immigrants. (The 2002 Farm Bill instituted a five-year waiting period for legal immigrants.) Coupled with the booming economy, the regulations led to significant enrollment declines throughout the 1990s.

In recent years enrollment has surged both in the Food Stamp Program and other hunger-relief measures in the United States, such as the supplemental nutrition program for women, infants, and children, known as WIC, and the National School Lunch and Breakfast Programs. Due to troubling studies published in the 1990s suggesting a connection between food stamps and obesity, recent reforms have helped shift the focus from providing a sufficient quantity of food to providing foods of high nutritional quality. One such reform was the 2008 Farm Act, which reauthorized the Food Stamp Program under the new name SNAP. The Farm Bill also included provisions that expanded eligibility and made it easier for participants to save their money. Most recently, due to high unemployment rates and the economic recession, President Barack Obama signed the American Recovery and Reinvestment Plan, in February 2009, to increase federal funding to SNAP and raise the minimum and maximum monthly allotments.

The pieces presented in this chapter ponder the role of food stamps and other programs in addressing the hunger problem in the United States. In "Hungry in America," Trudy Lieberman discusses the contrast between the United States' stated goal to offer its citizens "freedom from want" and the government's failure to properly address hunger. While Lieberman calls for expanding such programs as food stamps and WIC, she also argues that the only way to ultimately solve the problems of hunger and poverty is to enact a living wage and other reforms that address the needs of the working poor. The second article, "Reflections on the Food Stamp Program," by Bonny O'Neill, a former Food Stamp Program employee, provides an overview of the initiative and how its focus has changed over the last several decades. Next Michele Ver Ploeg and Katherine Ralston examine the connection between the Food Stamp Program and obesity, in their entry "Food Stamps and Obesity," noting that in order to stretch their food dollar recipients tend toward inexpensive products that are high in fat and sugar. In "Food Stamps," a writer for *America* considers the program's shortcomings, noting that often the food stamps are not enough to keep a family from going hungry.

In "Hunger Hysteria," Robert Rector disputes the very notion of food insecurity in the United States and argues that the Food Stamp Program has had little to no positive impact on the food consumption of the poor, citing studies showing a link between poverty and obesity. The next article, by Margaret Andrews, describes the changes in the Food Stamp Program, or SNAP, as a result of the 2008 Farm Act. In "Improving Food Choices—Can Food Stamps Do More?" the writers examine several possible strategies for improving access to fresh foods for Food Stamp Program participants. In the final entry in this chapter, "Balancing Nutrition, Participation, and Cost in the National School Lunch Program," the authors offer an expansive analysis of the National School Lunch Program (NSLP), which feeds low-income students throughout the country.

Hungry in America[*]

By Trudy Lieberman
The Nation, July 31, 2003

I have no heart for somebody who starves his folks.—George W. Bush

Ellen Spearman lives in a trailer at the edge of Morrill, Nebraska, a tiny dusty town near the Wyoming state line. A few years ago she was a member of the working poor, earning $9.10 an hour at a local energy company. Then she got sick and had four surgeries for what turned out to be a benign facial tumor. New owners took over the company and told her she was a medical liability and could not work full time with benefits. For a while she worked part time without benefits until the company eliminated her position. So the 49-year-old single mother of five, with two teenage boys still at home, now lives on $21,300 a year from Social Security disability, child support and payments from the company's long-term disability policy she got as a benefit when she was first hired. That's about $6,000 above the federal poverty level, and too high to qualify for food stamps. But it is not enough to feed her family.

Food is the expendable item in a poor person's budget. With the need to pay for gasoline, car insurance, trailer rent, clothes, medicine and utilities, and to make payments on a car loan and $10,000 in medical bills, Spearman says three meals a day "take a back seat." She says she and her family eat a lot of rice with biscuits and gravy. Their diet is more interesting only when a local supermarket sells eight pieces of chicken for $3.99 or chuck roast for $1.49 a pound. "This country doesn't want to admit there's poverty," she says. "We can feed the world but not our own."

Spearman's predicament mirrors that of many Americans. While the most severe forms of malnutrition and starvation that prevailed through the 1960s have largely disappeared, some 33 million people live in households that aren't sure where their next meals are coming from—those whom policy analysts call the

---

[*] "Hungry in America" by Trudy Lieberman. Reprinted with permission from the July 31, 2003 issue of *The Nation*. For subscription information, call 1-800-333-8536. Portions of each week's *Nation* magazine can be accessed at http://www.thenation. com.

food insecure. And with poverty on the rise—the United States experienced the biggest jump in poverty in a decade in 2001, to nearly 12 percent of the population—their ranks are growing. At the end of 2002 the US Conference of Mayors reported a 19 percent increase in the demand for emergency food over the previous year. Food pantries, shelters, soup kitchens and other emergency food providers now serve at least 23 million people a year. "They are America's dirty little secret," says Larry Brown, who directs Brandeis University's Center on Hunger and Poverty. "They are hardworking have-nots who cannot pay the rent, medical bills, and still feed their families."

Food and hunger are a lens through which we see what America has become: a country indifferent to the basic needs of its citizens, one that forces millions of them to rely on private charity that is inadequate, inefficient and frequently unavailable. As people with low and middle incomes have lost their jobs, their families line up for handouts, something many thought they'd never have to do. Hunger exposes the casualties of the ever-widening income gap between the rich and the rest of the population, and the damage inflicted by a twenty-year campaign waged by right-wing think tanks and conservative politicians to defund and delegitimize government. That campaign, which has succeeded in returning the public's view of poverty to the Darwinian one that prevailed before the Progressive Era at the turn of the twentieth century, is emblematic of the right's assault on public programs, which has used the old-fashioned notion of personal failing as the vehicle for accomplishing its political goals. Indeed, few politicians now advocate for the hungry.

THE WAY WE WERE

Beginning in the 1930s and into the 1940s, when Franklin Roosevelt articulated his Four Freedoms, including the freedom from want, America made a commitment, if not always perfectly executed, to feed the less fortunate. To be sure, the commitment was to some extent self-serving, in that food programs were designed to use up the surpluses produced by American agriculture. Still, there was a recognition that people couldn't always help themselves, and over the following decades champions emerged in Congress to battle for the needs of hungry people. From Robert Kennedy etching the face of hungry kids into the American conscience during his widely publicized trips to Appalachia to George McGovern and Bob Dole fighting for food stamps on the floor of the Senate, politicians stood up to help the hungry, putting government resources behind school lunches; school breakfasts; WIC, which feeds pregnant women and young children; and child nutrition.

When the nutrition programs under the Older Americans Act were created in 1972, authorizing special food programs for the elderly, it was Richard Nixon who pushed for more funding. Throughout the 1970s few Americans would have disputed the idea that the federal government had a major role to play in feeding the hungry. "Hunger was a problem we came much closer to solving in the 1970s," says James Weill, president of the Food Research and Action Center. "Food stamps were more available, wages at the bottom were higher and there was less inequality."

But then came the Reagan Revolution, with its emphasis on cutting government and the taxes needed to support it. In 1981, when the Heritage Foundation published its first Mandate for Leadership, the right laid out its plan "to restrain the food programs" and reduce the federal government's role. Some of its proposals, like moving the functions of the Community Food and Nutrition Program to the states through block grants, have come to pass. That has meant less money, intensive competition among nonprofit organizations and ultimately less outreach and advocacy for the hungry.

In his speech accepting the Republican presidential nomination, Ronald Reagan coined the term "safety net." Implicit was the idea that like a trapeze artist who needed a safety net only to prevent rare catastrophes, government would help only those in dire need and that most of the time people could provide for themselves. Almost everyone, including many liberals, bought into the concept, which subtly shifted the purpose of social programs from assuring adequate living standards for all to helping the few who occasionally fell on hard times. Reagan attacked the legitimacy of food stamps by painting a picture of undeserving welfare queens who ate at the government trough while buying vodka with their benefits. That notion stuck, and public support for food programs waned.

Now conservatives are again on the attack. Last December in the *Washington Post* Outlook section, Douglas Besharov, director of the Project on Social and Individual Responsibility at the American Enterprise Institute, argued that the WIC program contributed to childhood obesity. He posited that real hunger is found "predominantly among people with behavioral or emotional problems such as drug addicts and the dysfunctional homeless," and he criticized liberal advocacy groups, unions and farmers for standing in the way of reform and modernization, code words the right often uses to build support for dismantling a program while making it seem like they're improving it. Conservative columnists and op-ed writers picked up his arguments. This year WIC and the child nutrition programs are scheduled for Congressional reauthorization. While there's no question Congress will reauthorize the programs, planting doubt about them increases the chance politicians will change the rules to make fewer people eligible. WIC is the golden child of the food programs. If it is tarnished, the rest will lose favor as well.

LESS MONEY, FEWER MEALS

Spending on the cluster of nine domestic food programs rose from $30.3 billion in 1982 to $42.7 billion in 1992 (in 2002 dollars). In the 2002 fiscal year it had fallen to $38.4 billion—less than 2 percent of the entire federal budget. Those numbers reflect drastic reductions over time—the Reagan Administration's cuts in 1981–82 and the cuts mandated by welfare reform in 1996—as well as modest funding increases between 1984 and 1993. "The cuts at the beginning of the Reagan Administration and the '96 cuts were far bigger than the modest increases in intervening years," says David Super, general counsel for the Center on Budget and Policy Priorities. "Funding has recovered partially but is well behind what it would have been had it not been for the cuts."

Food programs for the elderly have suffered a steep decline in federal appropriations after adjusting for inflation. In 2002 the government spent $716.5 million on home-delivered meals and on meals provided at senior centers. Ten years earlier it spent $767.4 million (in 2002 dollars), which explains why all over the country older Americans stay for months on waiting lists for a hot meal delivered to their door. The budget for New York City's home-delivered meals programs illustrates the federal government's fiscal retreat: Twenty years ago Washington funded 80 percent of the program and the city funded the rest. Today the federal government provides less than 20 percent, and city and private sources provide the balance.

Because food stamps are an entitlement, spending depends on how many people apply. Currently, that amount is about $22 billion, making food stamps by far the largest federal food program. Food stamps, which date back to 1939, have never been used by 100 percent of all people who are eligible. The high point came in 1994, when 75 percent of all eligible people were on the rolls; the low point was in 1999, when only 58 percent were getting help. "A golden era for the food-stamp program never existed," said Doug O'Brien, vice president of America's Second Harvest. There was a time, though, when government agencies, such as the now-defunct Community Services Administration, sponsored extensive outreach and advocacy programs with the goal of enrolling more people. But after the Heritage Foundation attacked its advocacy work in the early 1980s, enrolling more participants was no longer encouraged, remembers Charles Bell, a VISTA worker at the time.

Participation also depends on how hard states make the application process, and in the 1990s they made it very hard. Unfriendly rules requiring excessive verification, more frequent visits from caseworkers and the need to reapply in person, as well as pressure on the states to reduce their error rates, discouraged many from applying. California, New York and Texas have practically criminalized the process by requiring applicants to be fingerprinted, an action that automatically brands them as potential cheaters. It's hardly surprising that only about half of all eligible residents in those states get food stamps. Receiving food stamps has always carried a stigma—"It's an intentional thing that keeps the program small and saves money," says Agnes Molnar, a senior fellow at New York City's Community Food Resource Center. Food-stamp participation is rising again nationwide, but many states still discourage applicants. In New York City, despite a sharp increase in unemployment, food-stamp use actually dropped between 2001 and 2003. "Low-income people have walked away from the program," O'Brien says.

According to Mathematica Policy Research, the average monthly benefit is $185, but the actual amount varies by family size. For elderly people living alone the average benefit is $50, but for 35 percent of this group, the benefit is only $10 because medical expenses and rent are not high enough to offset their monthly income, usually less than $600 from Social Security's Supplemental Security Income. When Congress reauthorized the food-stamp program last year, a move to increase the minimum benefit to $25 failed. "Because of the obsolescence of the assumptions on which food-stamp levels are based, they are no longer sufficient to prevent or guarantee against hunger," says Janet Poppendieck, a sociology professor at Hunter College in New York City. The food-stamp program assumed that families had 30 percent of their income to spend on food, an estimation that was more realistic when there was a much larger supply of low-income housing. Food stamps were intended to fill in the gap between the 30 percent and the cost of an arbitrarily set thrifty food plan. But today poor families use 50-80 percent of their income on housing and have far less to spend on food. The food stamps they do get are not enough for an adequate diet. So families run out of food before the month ends. That's when they turn to the 50,000 food pantries and soup kitchens across the country, links in an intricate system of food rationing that began as a temporary response to cuts during the Reagan years.

PANTRIES AS A WAY OF LIFE

Emergency food is now entrenched in nearly every city and town. It represents a fundamental failure of government to adequately feed its citizens. About 30 percent of the people who visit pantries receive food stamps—a stark indication that even those who do get stamps need more help and that many who need help are not getting them. The pantries' very existence lulls the public and politicians into believing they are the answer. But neither politicians nor anyone with adequate income would care to shop at them.

Food pantries are community supermarkets in poor neighborhoods. But shoppers can't come and go as they please, nor can they always choose the food they want. "Sometimes your heart can run away with your funds, especially when there are children involved," says Roy Lawton, a program director at Panhandle Community Services in western Nebraska. So, he adds, there must be limits. At his agency in Gering, people can come three times a year if they qualify. A family of four can have an income no greater than $23,920. If they have one dollar more, or if they've come too often, pantry workers send them to area churches that have less stringent rules.

The quantity of food people get is almost always restricted in some way. At Bread for the City in Washington, DC, workers simply hand clients a food bag after a computer check verifies that they have visited only once during the month. There's no choice of foods here. Food director Verneice Green explains that it would be "too chaotic" to let people in the back room, where the food is stored.

At St. Paul of the Shipwreck in San Francisco, the pantry resembles a child's board game. At each stop along a room lined with shelves, a person can choose a set number of items according to a color code and family size. At the West Side Campaign Against Hunger in Manhattan, director Doreen Wohl wants her pantry to resemble a supermarket so clients feel better about taking handouts. The currency here are points assigned to each item. A four-person family can take ten points' worth of food from each of the protein, vegetable, fruit and dairy sections, while a two-person family is allotted six points. On a busy Wednesday 280 people wheel shopping carts through the aisles, but the shelves are not well-stocked. There was less emergency food from the federal government than Wohl had expected—74,000 pounds less this year from the so-called TEFAP program.

At the pantries, people get hand-me-down food. It comes from supermarkets where it has stayed on the shelf too long or is damaged, or it comes from manufacturers that have produced too much of one item or made some product that didn't sell, like a cereal named Buzz Blasts or a soft drink that's blue. "Blueberry cola looks like windshield washer fluid, but in food banking, you take the good with the bad," says Bernie Beaudreau, director of the Rhode Island Community Food Bank. Castoff food, however, doesn't always make for the most nutritious diets, and arguably contributes to the diet-related health problems prevalent among the population forced to use food pantries. Amtrak has been a big supporter of the New England Shelter for Homeless Veterans in downtown Boston, and many of the 300,000 meals the shelter serves each year revolve around Italian wraps and sausage, egg and cheese breakfast sandwiches donated by Amtrak. "It's a struggle to provide a steady, nutritionally balanced diet, because of our reliance on donated food," says a shelter worker. Fresh meat and produce are often scarce at the pantries. Last fall in Lincoln, Nebraska, the Lincoln Action Program had enough ten-pound boxes of hamburger for the 400 to 600 people who were coming every week for food, and one day 300 clients lined up for onions, squash, apples and eggplant. But, says outreach worker Sheryl Haas, "there are weeks when the pickings are really slim."

They will grow slimmer as major changes sweep through the emergency food system. Many of the 216 food banks across the country that supply the pantries have less donated food to give away, particularly canned and boxed products that were once the food banks' staples. "Cereal donations are down 30–40 percent or more," says Frank Finnegan, who heads the St. Louis Area Food Bank. Mike Gillespie, who manages the warehouse for the Capital Area Food Bank in Washington, DC, used to get a call once a month from Giant Food to pick up excess products, but now, he says, Giant hasn't called in months. In 2000 Giant gave the food bank about 2.5 million pounds of food. Last year its donation fell to 1.6 million pounds.

Ironically, food banks have caused supermarkets, manufacturers and restaurants to become aware of how much food they were giving away. With the help of scanning technology and just-in-time inventory systems, businesses changed their practices. At the same time, more outlets such as Super Wal-Marts, dollar stores and flea markets have sprung up where manufacturers can sell their products. Although they get tax breaks for donating, food companies would rather sell than donate.

The only bright spot is that more produce is available because food-bank managers have aggressively sought donations of fruit and vegetables, and major donors have given money so perishables can be shipped quickly around the country. Yet many pantries don't have adequate refrigeration, or they are staffed with elderly volunteers who can't lug around 100-pound bags of onions and potatoes.

Some food companies have embraced "cause marketing," a new kind of charity that ties a firm's brand with a warm, fuzzy cause like hunger. "It's doing well for the company and doing good at the same time," explains Carol Cone, CEO of Cone Communications in Boston. But cause marketing hardly begins to solve the needs of hungry people. With Cone's help, the giant ConAgra Foods supports some of the 900 Kids' Cafes around the country—including one of the twenty-eight in Washington, DC, that serve 1,200 kids out of 43,000 children who are eligible. Other individuals and groups try to fill in the gaps. Last year Washington Wizards owner Abe Pollin raised $1 million to pay for 680,000 meals during the summer, a time when supplies at food pantries run low and school breakfasts and lunches are not available. But when the money ran out, the meals stopped.

Underlying the premise of food banks was the notion that someday they would not be needed and would disappear. Instead, food banking has become big business. Pantries have proliferated, there are jobs to protect, salaries to pay, an infrastructure to maintain. Perhaps as a result, there's a split among food-bank leaders, with some believing they should advocate for government solutions to the fundamental problems of poverty and others believing that rounding up more donations is the answer. Some food-bank boards of directors are fearful of direct advocacy. "We've chosen not to get involved politically," says Finnegan. But, he says, "private industry is not going to be able to solve this problem. If it's anyone's responsibility, it's the government's."

GETTING TO ROOT CAUSES

Hunger, of course, is symptomatic of a deeper problem—inadequate income, which hits even the US military at a time when the country has chosen guns over butter. The WIC office located at Offutt Air Force base near Omaha serves 650 servicewomen, wives of military personnel and their children each month. To qualify for free food, a family of three, for example, must have a gross income this year that's less than $28,231. "Most people don't have enough money. That's why they're in the program," says a WIC official. Through the years, however, feeding people through special programs rather than dealing with their lack of money became the palatable political choice.

Those who favor the route of special programs say it would not take a lot of money to insure that all Americans are fed. "Six billion dollars more could cut hunger in half in two years," says David Beckmann, president of Bread for the World. "It's an eminently solvable problem." But more government money is not likely. In fact, there will probably be less. Earlier this year House Republicans passed legislation that would transform the food-stamp program into a block grant, yet another way of pushing responsibility to the states and letting them decide when and if they have sufficient revenues to feed people. It's a way of converting an entitlement into revenue streams for states. After a few years they can divert money to other programs. It's not hard to imagine what will happen to the needy if the recession and budget deficits continue for several years. At the same time, the Agriculture Department hopes to make it more difficult to qualify for free and reduced-price school lunches, because, it says, some kids are getting cheap lunches even though their families are not eligible. Data, however, show that when more income documentation is required, it reduces participation among eligible children.

Today it's hard to find a champion for the hungry in Congress, much less in the executive branch. Hunger is not seen as a pressing political problem. In January, representatives of food advocacy groups met with Agriculture Secretary Ann Veneman and were told there were no extra dollars for food. "We were told it's going to be a tight budget year," says Beckmann. "They said there would be no more money for child nutrition, and we had to think about how to do more with the money we've got." Robert Blancato, a food-advocacy group lobbyist, says food programs must be recast to generate Congressional interest. "In this environment, programs need additional buzzwords to survive," he says. "If you can repackage the meal programs so they don't look like meal programs, they have a better chance. There's a whole new priority structure in where the money is going."

Meanwhile, no one in Washington talks much about living wages, increasing the minimum wage, indexing it for inflation or expanding the earned-income tax credit. But living wages are the only solution if people are ever to move toward the self-sufficiency and personal responsibility that politicians and the public demand of them. It's hard to buy food when the money you have goes for ever-increasing shelter costs, healthcare because you have no insurance and childcare because there are few low-cost options.

No modern industrial nation should protect the nutritional well-being of its citizens through handouts. But until an outraged public decides that hunger is unacceptable in the richest country in history, there will be more Ellen Spearmans asking why they cannot feed their families.

Reflections on the Food Stamp Program[*]

By Bonny O'Neil
Policy and Practice of Public Human Services, June 2004

While the volatile nature of the Food Stamp Program (FSP) allows almost any year to be claimed an anniversary year of some sort, 2004 is at least a triple-header. It marks the fortieth anniversary of the law that made the pilot programs of the early 1960s permanent and the thirtieth anniversary of nationwide implementation. The first Electronic Benefit Transfer (EBT) pilot began in Reading, Pennsylvania, twenty years ago, and during this past year the last food coupon rolled off the presses—bringing the program fully into the electronic age of debit and smart cards.

THE EARLY PROGRAM

When I entered government work in 1968 as a U.S. Department of Agriculture (USDA) food stamp novice, the dominant feeding program was still distribution of donated food directly to the poor. Counties wanting a food stamp program were placed on a waiting list until funds became available for them to switch over. Some 300 counties had no food program at all. Eligibility was based on state-by-state public assistance income rules. Participants were expected to buy the portion of their allotment that represented what they would spend on food without the program and they received a bonus to make up the difference between that amount and what they needed to buy a more adequate diet.

The amount of the subsidy varied between the North and the South, and while those with the least income received a higher percentage bonus, they still got less than was needed for a nutritionally adequate diet. These policies reflected a fear that the disproportionate amount of "money" for food, in a time when welfare grants were woefully inadequate, would put irresistible pressure on people to sell their food coupons to pay for other basic needs such as rent or shoes for the kids.

The purchase price was important because it assured that people would in fact spend more for food than they had spent previously—it would provide them with better nutrition and it would provide additional revenue to the commercial sector. One of the criticisms of the commodity programs was that people used the commodities to substitute for the money they would have spent on food in grocery stores, thereby freeing up their cash to spend on other items.

Isabelle Kelley, an agricultural economist, one of the four-person team that designed the pilot program in the early sixties, and its first director observed that ". . . the food stamp program flies in the face of rational economic behavior of consumers—that consumers would be willing to take one element of the standard of living and increase it to 100 percent of efficiency and leave all the rest of the elements . . . at substandard levels, and that they would be happy about it."

RICHARD NIXON TO THE RESCUE?

In a eulogy last year to former USDA Secretary Dick Lyng, USDA Secretary Ann Veneman related that she had asked him what in his long and distinguished career had made him most proud. There were many possibilities but she thought the most likely choice would be his accomplishments in the trade arena. Instead, he surprised her by saying that he was most proud of the improvements he had made in FSP in the late 1960s and early 1970s when he had been a USDA assistant secretary. In retrospect, it is not surprising that he picked that time and this program although most people might expect Ronald Reagan's secretary of Agriculture to look elsewhere for career achievements.

According to Kelley, advocates brought into the social arena by the War on Poverty and the civil rights movement saw FSP as a basis for a federally funded general assistance program. It was easy for them to ridicule the state-by-state eligibility levels and to highlight the large number of eligible people who did not take part in the program because of the purchase price. She noted that the struggle for civil rights and the war on poverty helped create an environment in the late sixties that was ready for social reform. "Hunger in America," which aired on CBS in 1968, the Poor People's March on Washington, and the 1967 Field Foundation study by a group of doctors who visited and documented extreme hunger and malnutrition in the poorest counties in the country all converged at about this time.

It was an exciting time. Lyndon Johnson's efforts at reform had been sidetracked by the Vietnam War and a new president, Richard Nixon (who would later face a similar choice and outcome), was ready to surprise his critics by naming Patrick Moynihan as his domestic policy advisor and boldly calling for a cash assistance program that would provide a monthly income guarantee for all families. On a parallel track, in December 1971, Nixon convened the first White House Conference on Food, Nutrition, and Health, which was attended by over 3,000 people. And, he pledged publicly to "put an end to hunger in America." In a follow-up report on the conference, the administration stated its intention to convert FSP into a cash program, move it to what is now the Department of Health and Human Services, and provide better coordination with "other income maintenance programs." Ironically, it might be argued that today's FSP provides the income floor that Nixon had hoped to create as part of his Family Assistance Plan.

Meanwhile, USDA undertook major liberalizations to existing food programs. The FSP purchase price was lowered, national standards of eligibility were enacted, and the amount of food stamps received now equaled the cost of a nutritionally adequate diet. As a result of these changes and additional congressional funding, there was major program growth. When I started in 1968, 3.6 million people participated in FSP and its budget was $248 million. By 1971, the program was serving 9.3 million people at a cost of $1.2 billion. That same year, legislation passed mandating national eligibility standards. Three years later in 1974, another law mandated that all states must have FSP in every county. No wonder Secretary Lyng was so proud of this period in his life when such monumental changes in social policy occurred.

THE LATE 1970s, 1980s, AND 1990s, OR PROOF THAT

THE PENDULUM THEORY IS REAL

In 1977, the modern FSP was created through major statutory liberalizations, the most significant of which was eliminating the purchase requirement. That one change added about 3.5 million people to the program. For historical accuracy I should note that the seventies were not all rosy for FSP. The Ford years were among the most difficult for the program as efforts were made by some to effectuate massive cuts through legislation and later through regulation. Fortunately, the courts had other ideas and those highly questionable regulatory efforts died when the Carter Administration took over.

There is no way I can do justice to the significance of the 1977 law and its implementation so I will simply say that the Carter years, under the leadership of Assistant Secretary Carol Foreman and Food and Nutrition Service (FNS) Administrator Bob Greenstein, were the highlight of my government career in terms of their vision and raw commitment to making the goals of FSP come to life.

The 1980s and 1990s, with some modest exceptions, brought with them program cuts and retrenchments that culminated in the 1996 welfare reform legislation. The FSP was mercilessly raided and the restrictions on immigrants and time limits for the able bodied (even those who would work if work were available) were put in place. For years I was proud to talk about FSP as one program that had no major categorical restrictions—if you were poor, you were eligible. Immigrant and Able-Bodied Adults Without Dependents (ABAWD) policies, among others, make it difficult to make that claim today.

I believe that FSP should serve all who are financially in need. I believe a work requirement—a job, training, or public service—should be a condition of eligibility but only if an opportunity to work really exists. The work requirement may not always be funded at the most meaningful level, but it is a litmus test that potential recipients should be willing to pass. If the program can provide real training and jobs, that is great, but I have never thought of that as a basic mission and I would not push for it. I believe that a food program should be concerned with food needs, not with addressing the shortcomings of other parts of civil society. Too often policy has been made because one instance of abuse caused a national policy change. That change then complicates the program and denies benefits to a class of people who need our help. Our attempts to whittle out potential abuses have consistently resulted in unwarranted administrative complexities. Why in the world are we asking on application forms, "are you a fleeing felon?"

Most of my peers have heard me complain over the years that too much policy is made because people know, or think they know, of one case where someone got away with something. The search for loopholes and ways to fix them is something we just do not seem able to resist. If I could, I would do away with the vehicle resource test as many states do now under an option for consistency in the Temporary Assistance for Needy Families program. That welfare Cadillac just isn't in the budget of someone with income below the poverty level. We can all come up with our favorites in the law, or regulations. Our efforts to balance targeting benefits to individual situations (whether to curb an abuse or correct an anomaly) and the complexities that accompany it are not new, and no doubt will continue, but we need to continually remind ourselves of the consequences.

The examples I have used stem largely from the more conservative efforts to address program abuses, but those on the other end of the spectrum have a lot to answer for as well when it comes to complexity. All too often, administrative complications are ignored in favor of relatively small gains. Standard utility allowances, notice after notice, office hours, and staffing standards are just a few past examples. The strategy is to get these protections into law or regulation when your folks are in charge because it is very difficult for a new administration to change the status quo. It is hard to take something away without severe criticism and it takes time for most administrations to figure out the cumbersome regulatory process.

I was privileged to work for almost 35 years with people committed to making FSP work. They are not all policy wonks nor are they "food stamp groupies" or technocrats. They value the program for its role as our nation's social safety net. It is not the solution for eliminating poverty but it is one of the most significant efforts available to us today to address the needs of the poor. There is still a lot of work to do and whether FSP continues to fill the gap, or becomes unnecessary because more comprehensive solutions are found, remains to be seen. Meanwhile, we should be proud to live in a nation that is committed to ending hunger and helping those in need.

Food Stamps and Obesity[*]

What We Know and What It Means

By Michele Ver Ploeg and Katherine Ralston
Amber Waves, June 2008

Critics of the Food Stamp Program point to higher rates of obesity among some low-income populations and question whether the program might have been too successful in boosting food consumption. They assert that giving assistance in the form of benefits redeemable for food, instead of cash, has led participants to spend more on food and eat more than they would have otherwise. Others wonder if the monthly issuance of food stamp benefits is linked to boom-and-bust cycles of consumption that could lead to weight gain over the long term.

A recent ERS [Economic Research Service] report explores whether there is any evidence of a causal link between food stamp participation and obesity. ERS reviewed and synthesized the growing and sometimes conflicting research on the issue. Researchers placed greater weight on studies that used statistical methods to control for the fact that people choose to participate in the program and those who participate are likely to be different from those who do not in ways that researchers cannot always observe. These differences could be related to body weight.

The weight of evidence from these studies indicates that for most program participants, food stamp benefits do not increase either Body Mass Index (BMI—a measure of weight adjusted for height) or the likelihood of being obese. A review of the research indicates that food stamp benefits do not increase the likelihood of being overweight or obese for men or children. For nonelderly adult women, who account for 28 percent of all food stamp participants, multiple studies show a potential link between food stamp receipt and an increase in obesity and BMI, although this effect appears to be small—about 3 pounds for a woman 5'4" to 5'6" tall. Some studies found that long-term participation in the program appears to heighten the impact on obesity.

---

[*] *Amber Waves* is published by the Economic Research Service (ERS), U.S. Department of Agriculture.

It is not clear why participation in the Food Stamp Program may increase the probability of obesity for women but not for men or children. Research about the causes underlying these results is not conclusive. Differences in energy requirements, activity levels, and eating patterns could be possible explanations. Because the Food Stamp Program is administered as a household-level program, devising program changes that are appropriately targeted to household members who may be at risk of gaining weight, without harming those who are not and need the nutritional assistance, is a challenge. Policy changes that help program participants improve their overall diets or help them "smooth" their food consumption over periods of high and low income may be more effective. For example, issuing food stamp benefits on a biweekly, or even weekly basis, may help food stamp participants obtain and consume food on a more even basis.

TOO MUCH MONEY FOR FOOD OR TOO INFREQUENTLY ISSUED?

The Food Stamp Program is an entitlement program available to all U.S. households that meet the eligibility requirements pertaining to income, assets, work, and immigration status. Program benefits can be used to purchase almost any food sold by participating food retailers, except for food prepared in the store, hot foods, and alcohol and tobacco. The average monthly benefit level in 2007 was $96 per person and $215 per household, which translates roughly to $3.20 per person per day or $7.16 per household per day to spend on food. Most program participants spend some of their own money on food in addition to their monthly food stamp allotment.

There are two leading explanations for how food stamp benefits could contribute to weight gain that may lead to obesity. The first argues that restricting food stamp benefits to food purchases results in participants spending more money on food and thus consuming more food than they otherwise would if they did not participate in the program. Although food stamp benefits may have the intended effect of reducing undernourishment or underweight for at least some participants, this explanation implies that the benefits may also be pushing a portion of participants into overweight or obesity. If true, then one solution is to deliver food stamp benefits as cash. Cash benefits have been found to induce smaller increases in food spending than benefits that can be spent only on food.

But even if receiving food stamp benefits leads participants to spend more on food, it does not mean that the additional spending results in overconsumption and obesity. It is possible that food stamp benefits allow people to choose a different bundle of foods than they otherwise would. For example, participants may shift spending toward relatively more expensive foods that were previously out of reach (e.g., fresh meats versus canned beans or fresh fruit and vegetables instead of canned items). Or, since food stamps can be redeemed for food only in grocery stores, participation in the program may shift a household's food spending toward foods prepared and consumed at home, as opposed to food away from home, in either case, an increase in food expenditures would not necessarily lead to over-consumption of calories or a poorer diet.

The food stamp cycle explanation argues that the practice of distributing food stamps only once a month results in alternate periods of under- and overconsumption, a pattern dubbed the "food stamp cycle," which may result in weight gain. Households consume food every day but purchase food less regularly—every few days for some households, every few weeks for others. It is possible that food stamp participants run out of food (and benefits with which to purchase more food) near the end of the month. As food becomes scarce and food intake is restricted, a person may lose weight. Then, when food is abundant, the individual may overeat. This distorted pattern of consumption with its periods of binge eating gradually can lead to increased weight.

TEASING OUT CAUSE AND EFFECT

Two conditions can be associated with each other, without one being the cause and the other the effect. Food stamp benefits may be associated with increases in body weight but may not cause greater body weight if something else is to blame. Determining cause and effect is difficult because no experiments have been conducted comparing the body weights of participants randomly assigned to receive program benefits with those of others assigned to a comparison program (or lack of a program). Researchers must instead rely on nonexperimental methods that try to determine what would have happened if no one received food stamp benefits or if an alternative program to food stamps was implemented.

Comparing body weights of food stamp participants with those of eligible non-participants is an obvious starting point, but this approach may be problematic. Food Stamp Program participants may have different characteristics than those who are eligible for the program but choose not to participate. Very poor individuals, for example, may be more likely to participate than individuals who are less poor but still eligible. A household with a strong preference for food relative to other necessities may be more likely to apply for food stamps than an otherwise similar household. This strong preference for food may also lead to weight gain that would have occurred whether or not the household participated in the program.

While most studies try to control for as many differences between participants and nonparticipants as possible, it is likely that important differences are not observed. If these differences are related to body weight, then the estimated effects of food stamp participation could be biased. This bias is called selection bias because individuals self-select into the Food Stamp Program. Researchers note that poverty is associated with higher risk of obesity in some population subgroups (for example, white women), but lower risk in others (among Black and Hispanic men), suggesting that selection bias can be positive or negative in the case of food stamp participation and obesity. Accounting properly for selection bias can reveal a higher or lower risk of obesity than estimates that do not account for such bias.

ERS researchers reviewed over a dozen studies of the relationship between food stamp participation and BMI and the likelihood of obesity. Several of the earlier studies used cross-sectional data (observations of many individuals for a single point in time) and controlled for observed factors that might be related to body weight, such as age, race, sex, and education. While these studies are useful for understanding broad trends and highlighting possible relationships for further exploration, they do not account for potential selection bias and only observe individuals at a point in time, so they are of limited use in drawing causal conclusions.

The ERS review focused primarily on studies that attempt to control for selection bias (often using longitudinal data with multiple observations on the same individuals) and which are better able to tease out cause and effect between food stamp participation and weight. One can never be sure that these methods are truly picking up cause and effect, but the methods used in these studies help researchers get closer to that goal.

DIVERSE EFFECTS REFLECT DIVERSE PARTICIPANTS

The Food Stamp Program serves a diverse population. In 2006, children accounted for almost half of all participants. Working-age women made up 28 percent of the caseloads, working-age men 13 percent, and the elderly age 60 and older 8 percent. Most of the food stamps issued go to households containing a child, elderly adult, or nonelderly disabled person (89 percent of all benefits). Many of the households receiving food stamps are single-adult households with children (34 percent). The ERS review of the effects of food stamp participation on body weight for this diverse group of participants found that food stamp participation has a small effect on obesity for adult women, but not for men or school-age children. Only a few studies have looked at children younger than 5 and the elderly, and they did not control for selection bias, so these subgroups are not discussed here.

Results for children ages 5–12 vary across sexes and differ in the direction of the relationship between food stamp participation and body weight. For young boys, studies found either no relationship between food stamp participation and BMI, or that food stamp participation is linked to a lower probability of being overweight (BMI-for-age greater than or equal to the 95th percentile).

For young girls, some studies found no association between food stamp participation and BMI. One study found that additional years of food stamp participation were associated with greater probability of being overweight. Another found a negative relationship between food stamp participation and being at-risk of overweight (BMI-for-age greater than or equal to the 85th percentile). These two studies used different methodologies, which could account for the disparate results.

For adolescent children (ages 12–18), food stamp participation does not seem to be related to BMI or the probability of being overweight. None of the reviewed studies found a link between program participation and body weight for teenage boys or girls.

Only one reviewed study found a significant link between food stamp participation and BMI, overweight, or obesity status for men ages 19–59. That study found that food stamp participation by men was positively related to BMI but not to overweight or obesity. Previous studies comparing average BMI for men across food stamp participation and income levels found that for some racial and ethnic groups, food stamp participants had lower BMI than income-eligible nonparticipants and higher income men. In view of that, it is possible that either the positive effect of food stamps on BMI was not large enough to shift more men into the overweight (BMI greater than 25) and obese (BMI greater than 30) categories, or the shift in BMI was an improvement among underweight men.

Adult (ages 19–59) women are the only food stamp participants for which multiple studies show a link between food stamp participation and overweight. Not all studies showed that participation affects body weight. However, results from studies that used different techniques to control for selection bias indicate that food stamp participation may increase the probability that a woman is obese. The estimated 2- to 5-percentage-point change in the probability of being obese translates into a 5- to 21-percent increase in obesity rates. Other results show that food stamp participation is associated with an estimated 0.5-point increase in BMI for women, or about 3 pounds for a woman between 5'4" and 5'6" tall.

OVER LONGER PARTICIPATION, EFFECTS MAY ACCUMULATE

The reviewed studies showed a stronger connection between long-term food stamp participation on body weight than short- or medium-term participation. Two studies found that women who received food stamp benefits for longer periods of time (one study defined "long term" as at least 2 consecutive years, the other as up to 5 consecutive years) increased the probability of being obese by 4.5 to 10 percentage points, which translates into a 20- to 50-percent increase in obesity rates.

Evidence is mixed with respect to long-term food stamp participation and men's weight. One study found no relationship between long-term participation (up to 5 consecutive years) on BMI or the probability of obesity for men. A second study found that participation for at least 2 consecutive years increased BMI and the probability of obesity for men, but shorter and repeated participation did not have these effects.

Most food stamp participants receive benefits for less than a year—the median length of food stamp participation is 6 to 8 months. Some participants, however, cycle on and off food stamps and others participate for longer periods. It is possible that small but positive effects of current food stamp participation on BMI may accumulate over longer, or shorter but repeated, periods and result in substantial total effects on BMI over time. Or, if the causal mechanisms underlying weight gain for women are related to periods of boom and bust surrounding the monthly issuance of food stamp benefits, then prolonged food stamp use could result in long-term weight gain. Further research may be able to tell a clearer story.

IMPLICATIONS FOR THE TYPE AND TIMING OF BENEFITS

One hypothesis of how food stamp participation causes weight gain is that benefit amounts are too high, causing participants to spend more money on food and thus consume more food than they otherwise would. One of the reviewed studies showed that the effect of food stamp participation on obesity is larger for single women than for women residing in households with more than one adult. Other research found that food stamps have little impact on the amount of money single women spend on food (i.e., the benefit amount is at least as big as what they otherwise would have spent on food). In that case, "cashing out" food stamp benefits to reduce overconsumption may not have the intended effect on body weight. The group whose weight is most affected by food stamp participation would not change their food spending if the benefits were shifted to cash.

Some studies measured participation as a dichotomous yes-or-no condition, while others looked at the amount of benefits the household received. Studies that used the amount of benefits to measure participation found a less consistent relationship between food stamp benefit levels and obesity [than] those that used the dichotomous measure. So, while some studies suggest a relationship between food stamp participation and obesity among women in particular, the research does not clearly indicate that higher benefit levels are associated with greater BMI and obesity, or that lower benefits would lead to lower BMI.

None of the studies reviewed explicitly tested whether boom-and-bust food consumption patterns associated with the benefit payment cycle contribute to obesity. If further studies find a causal link between the timing of benefits and disrupted patterns of consumption, possible policy solutions could include either increasing the frequency of benefit payments (biweekly or weekly) or raising the benefit amount, which could, paradoxically, help reduce obesity by reducing hungry days at the end of the benefit cycle.

The stronger relationship between food stamp participation and body weight found for women but not for men, the mixed relationships found for young boys and young girls, and the lack of any relationships found for adolescents make it difficult to come up with appropriate changes to the program to address obesity. Most food stamp benefits go to households that contain a child, elderly adult, or nonelderly disabled adult. Devising program changes that are appropriately targeted to household members who may be at risk of gaining weight, without harming those who are not will be difficult. Nutrition education efforts and other programs that help improve the overall diets of all household members may be more effective.

Food Stamps[*]

America, July 30, 2007

Politicians pushing shopping carts down supermarket aisles are not an ordinary sight. But some in public office have been doing just that in accepting a weeklong challenge to experience the difficulties of living on a food stamp allowance of barely more than one dollar per meal. This year Congress must make its five-year reauthorization of the farm bill, and food stamps are part of it. Oregon's Governor Theodore Kulongoski accepted the challenge and found, during a week of living on what food stamps could buy, that he went to bed earlier because he was more tired at the end of the day. Nor is he the only one to find that benefits at their present levels do not provide enough food to stave off weariness and provide adequate nutrition. The reason lies partly in the program's inadequate funding, which is largely a consequence of benefit cuts imposed by the 1996 welfare law. Reauthorization now offers Congress the chance to remedy that unacceptable situation. That a number of members of Congress have themselves accepted the food stamp challenge has heightened public awareness.

The Department of Agriculture uses its Thrifty Food Plan to determine how much money a low-income household needs for a nutritious diet. But as anti-hunger advocates point out, the dollar amount called for by this plan is higher than the average food stamp benefit. In reality many families run out before the end of the month. Low-income shoppers, moreover, have little choice but to buy calorie-dense foods that assuage hunger but can lead to obesity. The more nutritious foods tend to be more expensive. The situation is all the more worrisome because over half of food stamp recipients are children.

Only 60 percent of those eligible for food stamps receive them. The reason lies partly in the complex application process, which can be daunting, especially for people of limited education. Lack of outreach help is also part of the reason for the low enrollment. Another barrier to eligibility is the resources test. Resources (cash on hand, checking and savings accounts, for example) may not exceed

$2,000, a limit that has remained unchanged for 21 years, with no adjustment for inflation. Advocates point out that the current limit is so low that households are practically forced into impoverishment before they can become eligible for food stamps. Reauthorization should include raising the resource limit.

Another needed change concerns legal immigrants, who are ineligible because of a mandatory five-year wait before they can apply. Legal immigrants should be given the same access to the program as U.S. citizens. Undocumented immigrants are never eligible, but their citizen children are. Because of language problems, however, and understandable fears of arrest and deportation, undocumented parents may be reluctant to apply for their children.

The farm bill's nutrition title includes the Commodity Supplemental Food Program. The administration's 2008 budget calls for its elimination, which would end nutritional assistance for almost half a million seniors and thousands of low-income women and children. The program provides them with monthly food boxes of nutrient-rich foods like tuna fish and canned fruits and vegetables. According to the nonprofit Center on Budget and Policy Priorities, a food package costs the government less than $20 per participant.

One positive step is a bill introduced by Jim McGovern (Democrat of Massachusetts) and Jo Ann Emerson (Republican of Missouri), co-chairs of the House Hunger Caucus, both of whom accepted the one-week food stamp challenge. Their bill, the Feeding America's Family Act, co-sponsored by over 80 other members of Congress, would add $4 billion to the food stamp budget and thereby increase benefit levels. It would also lift the absurdly low minimum food stamp allowance of $10 a month, set in 1977 and never indexed for inflation, to $32 a month—an amount that could prompt a single adult living alone to make the effort to apply. Moreover, it would allow higher deductions for child care expenses. Not least, it would allow former felony drug offenders, who are currently ineligible, to receive food stamp benefits, surely a needed change that would help them in the difficult transition from prison back to their communities. Finally, it also proposes to alter restrictive asset rules by excluding a family's savings for education and retirement funds.

Reauthorization of the farm bill, with positive legislation of this kind folded in, offers a chance to reshape what the U.S. bishops' conference has called our broken agricultural policies. The food stamp program represents a part of those policies that is important if the goal is to be reached of reducing the number of people—35 million—who are estimated to be "food insecure." In a country as rich as the United States, no one should have to go hungry or suffer from malnutrition.

Hunger Hysteria

Examining Food Security and Obesity In America[*]

By Robert Rector
National Review, November 21, 2007

This week, the U.S. Department of Agriculture (USDA) released its annual report on household food security in the United States. According to USDA, some 12.5 million households, or roughly 11 percent of all households, experienced "household food insecurity" at some point in 2006 and some 35 million people lived in households with some form of food insecurity. Most of these households were low income. The report showed little change in food security levels in the U.S. over the last decade.

While these numbers sound ominous, it is important to understand what "food insecurity" means. According to the USDA, "food insecurity" is usually a recurring and episodic problem rather than a chronic condition. In 2006, around two-thirds of food insecure households experienced "low food security," meaning that these households managed to avoid any disruption or reduction in food intake throughout the year but were forced by financial pressures to reduce "variety in their diets" or rely on a "few basic foods" at various times in the year. According to the USDA, the remaining one-third of food insecure households (around 4 percent of all households) experienced "very low food security," meaning that at least once in the year their actual intake of food was reduced due to a lack of funds for food purchase. At the extreme, about 1.4 percent of all adults in the U.S. went an entire day without eating at least once during 2006 due to lack of funds for food.

Children are generally shielded from food insecurity. Around one child in two hundred experienced "very low food security" and reduced food intake at least one time during 2006. One child in a thousand went a whole day without eating at least once during the year because the family lacked funds for food.

Political advocates proclaim that the USDA reports suggest there is widespread chronic hunger in the U.S. But the USDA clearly and specifically does not identify food insecurity with the more intense condition of "hunger," which it defines as "discomfort, illness, weakness, or pain . . . caused by prolonged involuntary lack of food."

What is rarely discussed is that the government's own data show that the overwhelming majority of food insecure adults are, like most adult Americans, overweight or obese. Among adult males experiencing food insecurity, fully 70 percent are overweight or obese. Nearly three quarters of adult women experiencing food insecurity are either overweight or obese, and nearly half (45 percent) are obese. Virtually no food insecure adults are underweight.

Food insecure men are slightly less likely to be overweight or obese than men who are food secure (70 percent compared to 75 percent). But food insecure women are actually more likely to be obese or overweight than are women who are food secure (73 percent compared to 64 percent).

Thus, the government's own data show that, even though they may have brief episodes of reduced food intake, most adults in food insecure households actually consume too much, not too little, food. To improve health, policies must be devised to encourage these individuals to avoid chronic over-consumption of calories and to spread their food intake more evenly over the course of each month to avoid episodic shortfalls.

Yet most proposed policy responses to food insecurity call for giving low-income persons more money to purchase food despite the fact that most low-income persons, like most Americans, already eat too much. Such policies are likely to make the current situation worse, not better. One commonly proposed policy, for example, is to expand participation in the Food Stamp program. Participation in the Food Stamp program, however, does not appear to reduce food insecurity. Households receiving food stamps do not have improved food security compared to similar households with the same non-food stamp income who do not participate in the program. Moreover, participation in the Food Stamp program does not appear to increase diet quality. Compared to similar households who do not receive food stamps but have the same non-food stamp income, households receiving food stamps do not consume more fruits and vegetables but do, unfortunately, consume more added sugars and fats.

While the Food Stamp program has little positive effect on food quality, considerable evidence indicates that the program has the counterproductive effect of increasing obesity. For example, a recent study funded by USDA found that low-income women who participate in the Food Stamp program are substantially more likely to be obese than women in households with the same non-food stamp income who did not receive food stamps. Over the long term, food stamp receipt was found to increase obesity in men as well. While other research has failed to confirm this link between food stamps and obesity, the possibility that this program has harmful effects remains quite real.

Developing a rational policy on nutrition and poor Americans will require dispelling common misconceptions concerning poverty and obesity. For example, one common misconception is that poor people become obese because they are forced, due to a lack of financial resources, to eat too many junk foods that are high in fat and added sugar. According to this theory, poor persons struggle to obtain sufficient calories to maintain themselves and are forced to rely on junk foods as the cheapest source of calories, but because junk foods have high "energy density" (more calories per ounce of food content), these foods paradoxically induce a tendency to overeat and thereby cause weight gain.

One problem with this theory is that junk foods are not a particularly cheap source of calories. For example, soft drinks are high in added sugar and are generally associated with weight gain, but as a source of calories, brand name soft drinks such as Coca-Cola and Pepsi are often more expensive (in terms of calories per dollar) than milk. Snack foods such as potato chips and donuts cost two to five times more per calorie than healthier staples such as beans, rice, and pasta. Families truly seeking to maximize calories per dollar of food expenditure would focus not on junk and snack foods but on traditional low-cost staples such as beans, rice, flour, pasta, and milk. These foods are not only less expensive but actually have below-average energy density and therefore a lower potential to promote weight gain.

In reality, poor people are increasingly becoming overweight for the same reason that most Americans are becoming overweight: They eat too much and exercise too little. Like the rest of America, the poor eat too many high-fat foods and foods with added sugars, but they do this for the same reason the average American over-consumes these foods: They are highly palatable. While it would be desirable for poor people (like all Americans) to drink fewer soft drinks and eat more broccoli, simply expanding the Food Stamp program would not accomplish that goal. What is required is a very difficult effort to change food preferences.

Contrary to the claims of poverty advocates, the major dietary problem facing poor Americans is too much, not too little, food. Public policies should be directed toward encouraging the poor to avoid chronic over-consumption, exercise more, and reduce intake of foods rich in fat and added sugar.

2008 Farm Act Makes It Easier for Food Assistance Households to Save[*]

Amber Waves, November 2008

USDA's Supplemental Nutrition Assistance Program (SNAP), formerly known as the Food Stamp Program, helps low-income households maintain a nutritious diet and meet other expenses when their budgets are strained. To qualify for benefits, however, households cannot exceed program-specified resource limits. Some households must first draw down their savings until their financial assets fall below program-defined limits.

The recently enacted Food, Conservation, and Energy Act of 2008 (Farm Act) includes new provisions that make it easier for participating households to save, especially for education or retirement. For the first time since they were set in 1985, the asset limits that determine program eligibility will be adjusted annually for inflation in increments of $250. The first change is expected to occur in 2012. Also, assets held in all tax-qualified retirement and education accounts (such as Individual Retirement Accounts (IRAs) and 529 Education Accounts) will not count against eligibility.

Currently, households with more than $2,000 in countable assets are excluded from participating in SNAP. (The limit is $3,000 if any household members are elderly or disabled.) Assets counted toward the limit include cash on hand, savings and checking accounts, stocks, bonds, and real estate not used as a home residence or for producing income. Automobiles worth more than $4,650 were countable, but by November 2007, all States had acted to exclude one or all personal vehicles or raise the exempted value.

ERS-funded research estimates that, in 2006, about 55 percent of households with incomes under 200 percent of the poverty level were eligible for food stamp benefits given then-existing income and asset requirements. The asset requirements had less of an effect on food stamp eligibility for households receiving

[*] *Amber Waves* is published by the Economic Research Service (ERS), U.S. Department of Agriculture.

Temporary Assistance for Needy Families (TANF) benefits than for households receiving Social Security benefits or with an elderly household member.

Eliminating asset limits altogether would have expanded food stamp eligibility by about 22 percent for the general population in 2006, but would not have appreciably increased eligibility for those receiving TANF. Based on 2006 data, an additional 354,000 households (slightly more than a 2-percent increase) will become eligible for SNAP benefits as a result of the 2008 Farm Act's exclusion of retirement accounts. Data were not available to estimate the effect of eliminating tax-qualified educational accounts.

In addition to increases in eligibility, the 2008 asset rules reduce disincentives to save that will affect not just the newly eligible, but future participants and the more than 28 million current participants. Although the effects of these changes on savings are difficult to estimate, the new asset rules are consistent with the goal of improving the self-sufficiency of low-income Americans.

Improving Food Choices—Can Food Stamps Do More?*

By Joanne F. Guthrie, et. al.
Amber Waves, May 2007

- Proposed strategies for improving diets of Food Stamp Program participants include restricting the types of foods purchasable with food stamp
benefits and offering bonuses or vouchers for buying healthful foods such
as fruits and vegetables.
- Offering bonuses or vouchers for specific foods essentially lowers their
price and gives the household additional income for food purchases.
- Prices and income can influence consumer spending decisions, but effective policies also need to account for the role of consumer preferences and
foods available in the marketplace.

When the Food Stamp Program began, its primary purpose was to enable low-
income Americans to get enough to eat, providing "stamps" usable only for food
but permitting each household its own choices of which foods to buy. Over time,
the program has changed from primarily focusing on getting a sufficient quantity
of food to an increased emphasis on also choosing healthful foods with high
nutritional quality. This reflects the nutrition-related health problems now facing
more and more Americans of all income levels. The prevalence of obesity and
diabetes is growing. Nutrition and health experts point to excessive intakes of
saturated fat and added sugars, coupled with low intakes of healthful foods such
as fruit, vegetables, and whole grains, as major contributing factors.

To help food stamp participants make more nutritious food choices, USDA
has expanded its investment in nutrition education. State governments and health
advocates are looking at additional modifications to the Food Stamp Program that
could reinforce nutrition education, including restrictions on the foods allowable
for purchase with food stamp benefits and expanded benefits to buy more of
healthful foods, such as fruit and vegetables.

The success of either restrictions or targeted benefits depends on a number
of economic factors: the food stamp budget share (the share of the food budget

* *Amber Waves* is published by the Economic Research Service (ERS), U.S. Department of Agriculture.

covered by food stamps); the food spending patterns of program participants; participants' response to changes in food prices and their response to increased income; and, finally, food manufacturers' response to Food Stamp Program changes. Research conducted by ERS on these economic factors provides insight into the likely effectiveness of these program modifications in improving the diets of program participants.

CAN LIMITING FOOD CHOICE IMPROVE DIETS?

Food Stamp Program benefit levels are set to allow households to purchase a set of low-cost foods that meet current Federal nutrition recommendations. Program benefits are provided through electronic debit cards that recipients can use to buy just about any foods sold in participating grocery stores, with the exception of hot prepared foods such as rotisserie chicken.

Restricting food stamp participants' purchases of foods and beverages high in calories, fats, and/or sugars has been proposed as a strategy to combat obesity. In 2004, the State of Minnesota unsuccessfully requested permission from USDA to prohibit the purchase of candy and soft drinks with food stamp benefits. The proposed modification was clearly intended to promote diet quality by limiting purchase of "empty calorie" foods.

While it may seem obvious that disallowing an "unhealthful" food item would necessarily limit its consumption, in practice such a policy may have limited effectiveness. The issue turns on whether food stamp recipients would continue to purchase the restricted items, using their own funds. This is likely to depend on the food stamp budget share. The larger the share of the food budget that is covered by food stamps, the more influence program changes can be expected to have. For most food stamp households, the food stamp budget share is a sizeable part of their food budget, but it is not the whole amount. For a family of four in fiscal year 2004, monthly benefit amounts varied from almost nothing to as much as $471, with the average benefit at $326. At the same time, a four-person, low-income household spent an average of $462 per month on food, including both food from grocery stores and food prepared away from home. Such a household could continue to buy at least some of the prohibited items with the $136 cash portion of its current food expenditures. Even if the cash devoted to foodstore purchases is relatively small under current policies, households might use some of their cash income currently being used for nonfood purchases to buy prohibited foods.

The impact of a food restriction will also depend on the amount of banned foods consumed by food stamp recipients. ERS research on food spending patterns shows that of the $462 spent on food each month by the average low-income, four-person household, $334 was spent on food from the grocery store. Of this, $11 was spent on sugars and sweets and $30 was spent on nonalcoholic beverages. Depending on how much of the spending in these categories is devoted to potentially prohibited items, such as candy and soft drinks, the average family might or might not be able to buy the same mix of foods using their cash resources. They might have to adjust their purchasing behavior to limit prohibited items and shift their food stamp purchases to other items.

But does it necessarily follow that they would shift to purchasing fruits and vegetables, low-fat milk, and other healthful foods? Consumers who love candy might choose the natural sweetness of fruit. Or they might switch to cakes, cookies, chocolate-coated granola bars, or any of a number of items that might have only minimal nutritional differences from banned items. In denying Minnesota's request for authority to ban certain candies, USDA noted that the request would prohibit the purchase of Hershey chocolate bars but allowed Kit-Kat and Twix candies (because they contain flour).

The effectiveness of limiting food choices also depends on food manufacturers' response. Limiting purchases of less-healthful foods might encourage manufacturers and retailers to develop more healthful products—like snack packs of baby carrots and pre-cut apple slices—and promote them more vigorously. Or food manufacturers and retailers might develop or promote sweets or snack foods very similar to the prohibited items. For example, they might develop a sweet, fruit-flavored drink that is very similar nutritionally to a prohibited soft drink.

Low-Income Households of Four Spend $54 Per Month on Fruit and Vegetables

	Average spending for a household of four, 2004-05			
Food expenditures	Low-income ($10,000-$29,999)	Middle-income ($30,000-$49,999)	Higher-income ($50,000 and more)	All
	Dollars per month			
Total food spending	462	527	816	700
Food away from home	129	195	374	298
Food at home	334	332	441	402
Meat/poultry/fish and seafood	91	86	105	100
Fruit and vegetables	54	50	71	64
Cereals/bakery products	46	46	61	56
Dairy products	38	40	51	46
Sugars/sweets	11	10	17	15
Fats/oils	10	10	11	10
Nonalcoholic beverages	30	31	40	37
Miscellaneous	52	56	81	72

Note: Amounts may not add up due to rounding.
Miscellaneous includes frozen and canned meals and soups; chips, nuts, and other snacks; condiments, etc.
Source: Consumer Expenditures Survey, Bureau of Labor Statistics.

The U.S. food market is extremely dynamic, with more than 20,000 new food and beverage products introduced in 2006 alone. It is likely that the market would respond with both healthful, innovative products that nutritionists would applaud and products that differ little from banned items. In this dynamic food environment, implementing restrictions on foods allowable with food stamp benefits would require continually updating regulations, issuing guidance, and making specific decisions where necessary (for example, is this a prohibited candy bar or an allowable breakfast bar?). More detailed regulations regarding allowable foods also could make food stamp purchases more complicated both for program participants and for the stores that accept food stamps.

CAN EXPANDING BENEFITS FOR HEALTHFUL FOODS IMPROVE CHOICES?

Rather than restricting choice, another policy suggestion is to encourage positive choices through targeting food stamp benefits toward healthful but underconsumed foods. This might be particularly useful for fruits and vegetables, underconsumed foods for which a perceived high cost is a commonly cited barrier to increased consumption. In 2004–05, on average, low-income, four-person households spent $54 per month on fruit and vegetables, $17 less than higher income, four-person households. Furthermore, an ERS study found that in 2000, approximately 19 percent of low-income households bought no fruit or vegetables in any given week, compared with 9 percent of higher income households.

Food stamp benefits can be designed to increase fruit and vegetable consumption via vouchers redeemable for fruit and vegetable purchases, as is currently done in the WIC Farmers' Market Nutrition Program. Or bonuses tied to the purchase of fruit and vegetables can be offered to program participants. California has passed legislation to conduct a "Healthy Purchase" pilot program. Under this program, for every $1 of food stamps spent on fresh produce, participants will receive a specified portion back, as a bonus. These bonus or voucher approaches could be expected to influence food choice through a price effect—they effectively lower the price of the targeted food—and through an income effect—they give the participant additional income to spend on food.

California's approach of tying a bonus to fruit and vegetable purchases has the effect of lowering the cost of produce relative to other foods. If price is the barrier to fruit and vegetable consumption, lower prices should result in food stamp households' purchasing more of the "cheaper" fruit and vegetables. But how much more? This depends on the extent to which participants respond to changes in price, as well as the size of the price change. The more strongly food stamp participants react to lower prices, the larger the effect on diet quality.

Consumer response to price varies for different types of goods, and even different types of foods. ERS research indicates that demand for fruit and vegetables appears to be somewhat more responsive to lower prices than other food categories. For example, a 10-percent discount in the price of fruit and vegetables would be expected to increase the amount purchased by about 6 to 7 percent. Given that estimated fruit and vegetable consumption of the average food stamp participant is about 1.75 cups per day, a 20-percent reduction in the price of fruit and vegetables would be estimated to raise consumption to about 2 cups—an improvement, although still below the recommendation for typical adults of 3.5 to 5 cups per day. (The estimation procedure does not allow extrapolation beyond a 20-percent price reduction.)

Rather than offering a bonus, another approach could be offering participants a voucher that can be used only to buy fruit and vegetables, lowering their price to zero for participants. This approach offers an incentive even to those households currently buying little or no fruit and vegetables.

Lowering the cost of fruit and vegetables either by offering a bonus or by providing a voucher also provides participants with additional food income. Under the bonus scenario, the bonus income adds to overall food purchasing power. Under the voucher scenario, households would likely substitute the vouchers for some of the fruit and vegetable purchases they would have made with food stamps. Again, the result is to increase household income available for food purchases.

What effect will this increased income have on diet quality? It depends on the choices made—more fruit and vegetables, low-fat milk, or whole grains? Or extra sweets and high-fat snacks? Previous ERS research found that receiving food stamps led participants to consume larger amounts of added sugars and total fats, not fruit and vegetables. Coupling a fruit and vegetable incentive program with nutrition education may increase the likelihood that food stamp participants use additional income to make healthful choices. Also, to the extent that the program provides incentives for food manufacturers and retailers to develop and promote appealing fruit and vegetable options, this may influence choice. The California pilot program includes a plan to work with small stores in low-income neighborhoods to increase produce offerings and market them appealingly.

CHANGING CONSUMER PREFERENCES—THE ULTIMATE CHALLENGE

Given that poor diets exert heavy costs in increased medical expenditures and lost productivity, effective policies for promoting healthful food choices among the 26 million low-income Americans participating in the Food Stamp Program could yield considerable benefits. Currently debated options include both restrictive policies that would prohibit buying some less-nutritious foods with food stamps and policies that would target expanded benefits to purchase of selected healthful foods.

Whether policies aim to restrict or expand food stamp participants' choices, it is ultimately the choices participants make that will dictate success in improving diet quality. A restrictive policy may limit purchase of some less nutritious foods, but given America's diverse and dynamic food industry, it would still be up to the consumer to choose either more healthful products or ones that, although not restricted, are essentially similar to the prohibited item.

Expanding benefits for healthful foods such as fruit and vegetables would be likely to increase their purchase. However, given existing consumer preferences, the predicted increase may not be strong enough, by itself, to bring purchases up to levels in line with current dietary recommendations. The challenge of changing consumer preferences remains. Coupling targeted benefits with nutrition education may increase effectiveness, as could a response by food manufacturers and retailers that resulted in more attractive, highly promoted fruit and vegetable options.

USDA recognizes the challenge. As part of the 2007 farm bill, USDA has recommended strengthening the nutrition education component of the Food Stamp Program. In particular, USDA has proposed investing $100 million over 5 years to develop and test solutions to the rising rates of obesity. Potential approaches include providing incentives to food stamp participants to buy fruit and vegetables, as well as integrated nutrition education programs to promote healthful diets and physical activity. These efforts would include rigorous independent evaluations to identify effective ways to improve food choice.

NUTRITION EDUCATION REACHING OUT TO FOOD STAMP PARTICIPANTS

Food Stamp Nutrition Education (FSNE) is an optional component of the Food Stamp Program conducted via a partnership and joint funding between USDA and States. Between 1992 and 2006, total annual Federal spending for FSNE increased from $661,076 to $247 million, and State participation expanded from 7 States to all 50 States, 2 Territories, and the District of Columbia.

To operate FSNE, State food stamp offices subcontract with one or more FSNE-implementing agencies. More than half of these are the Cooperative Extension Service of the State's land-grant university. Other implementing agencies include State or Territorial health departments and other public organizations.

Implementing agencies have considerable flexibility in the types of educational activities they conduct. Activities range from small group classes and cooking demonstrations for adults, to classroom activities in schools serving predominantly low-income children, to public service announcements in media outlets that serve mostly low-income audiences. Within this broad range of activities, USDA requires that all education be behaviorally focused, with a goal of encouraging participants to voluntarily make healthful, economical food choices for themselves and their families.

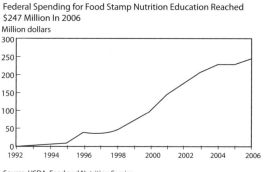

Federal Spending for Food Stamp Nutrition Education Reached $247 Million In 2006

Source: USDA, Food and Nutrition Service.

Balancing Nutrition, Participation, and Cost in the National School Lunch Program[*]

By Constance Newman, Katherine Ralston and Annette Clauson
Amber Waves, September 2008

The National School Lunch Program (NSLP) provides federally subsidized meals to more than 30 million children each school day. Recently, reported high rates of obesity and overweight among children have focused attention on the nutritional quality of school lunches. But this attention has raised another fundamental question: Can schools meet the program's nutrition goals while covering costs, especially in times of rising food prices?

School districts are responsible for providing school meals. They receive a per meal subsidy and free agricultural commodities from USDA to help operate school lunch programs. Schools also get revenues from NSLP meal sales to students who are not eligible for free meals. The costs of running the program can exceed these two revenue sources, and schools often turn to other funding or food sales to make up the difference. For many schools, calls to raise nutrition standards could mean higher costs. Some schools say that to satisfy students and keep up revenues, they may need to offer foods of lower nutritional quality.

While nationally representative data are not available, several case studies have found that schools can keep their budgets in the black while still serving nutritious lunches. Some have succeeded by reducing costs, and others have raised revenues through increased student participation. And schools have found creative ways to make healthy food appealing to students. Federal nutrition guidelines, meal reimbursement, and commodity donations can help schools meet their objectives, although variation in food prices and nutrition goals present added challenges.

* *Amber Waves* is published by the Economic Research Service (ERS), U.S. Department of Agriculture.

USDA PROVIDES PER MEAL SUBSIDIES AND COMMODITIES

USDA support is intended to cover much of the cost of providing NSLP lunches, and most of it is in the form of cash reimbursement for meals served. In 2007–08, USDA reimbursed schools $2.47 for each free lunch served, $2.07 for each reduced-price lunch, and $0.23 for each paid lunch. Basic Federal reimbursement rates are the same for all school districts across the country except in Hawaii and Alaska, which have higher rates to compensate for higher food prices in those States. Rates are also 2 cents more in districts where at least 60 percent of school meals are served free or at a reduced price. Reimbursement rates are adjusted by the Consumer Price Index for Food Away from Home for Urban Consumers once a year for inflation.

USDA also donates commodities to States to use in school lunches. In FY 2007, the commodities given to schools were worth 17 cents per meal for a total of $1.04 billion. Donation amounts vary per year, depending on availability and prices. States select from a wide variety of foods (including fruit and vegetables), based on what school food authorities need for their planned menus. The 2002 farm bill directed that USDA spend $200 million of entitlement funds for fruit and vegetables from 2002 through 2007, and the 2008 farm bill increased that amount to $406 million by 2012. In addition to the basic "entitlement" commodities, "bonus" commodities are sometimes available through USDA's price support and surplus removal programs.

The Fresh Fruit and Vegetable Snack Program is another program designed to increase fruit and vegetable availability to schools. Federal dollars are used directly by schools to purchase fresh fruit and vegetables for snacks. The 2008 farm bill called for a gradual expansion of this program to all States by 2012 and a total expenditure of $1 billion.

SCHOOLS FACE NUTRITION AND COST CONSTRAINTS

School food authorities (SFAs) face the dual constraints of meeting Federal nutrition requirements and covering operating costs. In many cases, SFAs must meet State and local nutrition requirements that are more stringent than Federal standards.

Federal law requires that NSLP lunches provide one-third of the Recommended Dietary Allowances for protein, vitamin A, vitamin C, iron, calcium, and calories. Schools can use a food-based meal pattern, in which certain types of foods must be served, or use a nutrient-based meal pattern that requires an entree and side dish that meet the nutrient regulations. Schools must offer a variety of milk with every meal, and this can be some combination of whole, 2-percent, 1-percent, skim, or flavored milk. Since 1996, Federal standards require that no more than 30 percent of meal calories can come from total fat and 10 percent from saturated fat when averaged over the school week.

States and local school districts, however, have been instituting their own stricter standards for years. In 2004, Congress called on SFAs to develop a "Local Wellness Policy," which would set goals for nutrition standards and physical activity. An estimated 33 States have instituted additional standards for school foods. Some States call for the complete removal of non-NSLP foods from cafeterias or campuses, while others restrict the times when non-NSLP foods are available.

Cost pressures present a challenge to improving the school food environment. The costs of producing school meals are rising, driven partly by higher health care costs for employees and recently by increasing food costs. Although Federal reimbursement rates are adjusted for inflation, some observers question whether the rates accurately track cost increases.

REPORT CARD: DO NSLP LUNCHES MAKE THE GRADE?

Studies show that students who get the NSLP meal have higher intakes of key nutrients (such as vitamins A, C, B6, folate, thiamin, iron, and phosphorus) than children who bring their lunches from home or buy a la carte items. Studies found that NSLP participants consume more milk and vegetables and fewer sweets, sweetened beverages, and snack foods than nonparticipants do at lunch, and the same trend holds for milk, vegetables, and candy over a 24-hour period.

In one study, NSLP participants were found to consume more calcium, fiber, fruits, and 100-percent juices, both at lunch and over 24 hours. The difference in intake between participants and nonparticipants was largest for calcium and was probably due to higher milk consumption for participants—about half a serving on average. The fact that differences were maintained over 24 hours indicates improvement in the overall daily diet, as opposed to improvement only at the lunch meal and counteracted at other meals.

Studies of nutrient intake also show similar calorie intake for participants and nonparticipants but higher fat and sodium intake for participants. Whether the higher fat intake extends to weight gain is not clear: One study shows no effect of school meal participation on children's obesity, and another study shows that NSLP participants have a 2-percentage-point higher probability of obesity.

Despite Federal regulations, many NSLP lunches do not actually meet fat and nutrient requirements. The most recently available data, the 2005 School Nutrition Dietary Assessment (SNDA), showed improvement in saturated fat content from the 1998–99 SNDA, but it found that only one in four elementary schools served lunches that met the standard for fat and one in three met the standard for saturated fat. For high schools, the numbers were even lower: 1 in 10 for fat and 1 in 5 for saturated fat.

THE FREE-MEAL SUBSIDY COVERS MOST, BUT NOT ALL, COSTS

In 2005–06, USDA's Food and Nutrition Service (FNS) sponsored a national study—the School Lunch and Breakfast Cost Study II—to evaluate the adequacy of reimbursements. The study measured cost in two ways: the reported cost and the *full cost* of producing a reimbursable or nonreimbursable meal.

Reported costs are those incurred by SFAs in providing meals; these costs are charged to their foodservice accounts. Full costs are the reported costs plus unreported costs that the school districts, not the SFAs, incur on behalf of the program. Unreported costs can include meal-time supervisory labor, administrative labor, such as that needed for payroll and accounting, as well as indirect costs, such as those associated with equipment and utility costs that are not charged to the SFA. In school year 2005–06, full costs were composed of food (37 percent), labor (about 48 percent), and other costs (about 15 percent), which included supplies, contract services, and indirect costs.

The FNS cost study found that in school year 2005–06, the average reported cost for producing a reimbursable lunch was $2.36 across SFAs. Summing the cash reimbursement for free lunches from that year ($2.32 and $2.34 for qualifying low income districts) and the entitlement commodity rate for that year ($0.175), the midpoint reimbursement rate was $2.51, which was higher than the average reported cost. Most schools had costs below the reimbursement rate: 78 percent of schools had reported per lunch costs that were below the USDA free-lunch subsidy rate.

Most Schools Meet USDA Nutrition Standards for NSLP Lunches Except for Total Fat and Saturated Fat

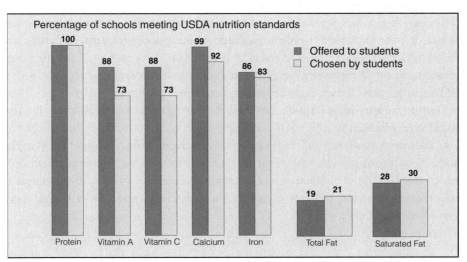

Source: USDA, Food and Nutrition Service. *School Nutrition Dietary Assessment-III, Menu Survey,* Nutrition Assistance Program Report Series, November 2007.

On the other hand, in school year 2005–06, the average full cost for producing a reimbursable lunch was $2.91 across SFAs, which is 40 cents higher than the midpoint free subsidy of $2.51. Only 32 percent of schools had full lunch costs that were below the USDA free-lunch subsidy. The finding that full costs are generally not covered by the free-meal rate points to the larger problem of hidden or, perhaps, unanticipated costs that can affect the long-term financial health of the program.

Schools with a larger share of students receiving free or reduced-price meals were likely to cover both types of costs. In schools where more than 60 percent of lunches served were free or reduced-price, revenues averaged 125 percent of reported costs and 107 percent of full costs. By contrast, in schools with less than 60 percent of free and reduced-price lunches served, revenues averaged 111 percent of reported costs and 88 percent of full costs. The greater amount of Federal subsidies received for those meals makes an important difference to schools in covering their costs.

SCHOOLS TURN TO COMPETITIVE FOODS FOR REVENUES

Revenues for school meal programs come from various sources: USDA subsidies, student payments for NSLP meals, sales of other foods, and State and local funds. According to the FNS cost study, 45 percent of revenues for the average SFA came from per meal reimbursements in 2005–06; 5 percent from commodity donations; 24 percent from student payments for NSLP meals; 16 percent from other food sales; and 10 percent from local and State government funds and other cash revenues. The sales of other foods have become a flash point for SFAs: The foods are less nutritious in general and yet their sales are considered necessary by many SFAs for financial survival.

These other foods, known as "competitive" or "nonreimbursable" foods, can include a wide variety of foods available at or near schools, including a la carte items sold in the cafeteria and snacks sold in vending machines. Vending machines were in 98 percent of senior high schools, 97 percent of middle/junior high schools, and 27 percent of elementary schools in 2004–05. A la carte items were available for sale in 75 percent of elementary schools and over 90 percent of middle and high schools.

Competitive foods are generally lower in key nutrients and higher in fat than the NSLP reimbursable meal. USDA requires only that "foods of minimal nutritional value" not be sold in foodservice areas during mealtimes. However, this requirement covers a limited number of foods, a small area of the school, and a short part of the day. The availability of competitive foods in a school has been found to reduce participation in NSLP, decrease nutrient intake from lunches, and increase the amount of food left uneaten and thrown away by students. The availability of unhealthy foods also sends a mixed message to students about the importance of nutrition.

Surprisingly, FNS's cost study finds that the revenues from nonreimbursable food sales do not cover their costs on average. Revenues from nonreimbursable foods covered less of their costs (both full and reported costs) than was the case for NSLP lunches. Revenues from NSLP lunches covered 93 percent of their full costs, compared with 61 percent for nonreimbursable meals. For reported costs, revenue from NSLP lunches covered 115 percent of costs versus 71 percent for nonreimbursable meals. Perhaps nonreimbursable sales serve other purposes for schools—such as attracting more students to the cafeteria. Or the costs incurred in selling nonreimbursable foods may be difficult to accurately separate from costs for reimbursable foods. The study assigns labor costs proportionately to the costs of nonreimbursable and reimbursable foods, and this may explain why the costs for nonreimbursable foods seem higher than expected.

BUILDING A HEALTHY SCHOOL LUNCH PROGRAM

The available evidence, while limited, suggests that nutrition and financial health do not have to conflict. A study of SFAs in Minnesota found that meal costs were not higher for cafeterias that met regulations for nutritional quality than for those that did not. Some, but not all, SFAs in a pilot study in California were able to improve nutritional quality while continuing to break even.

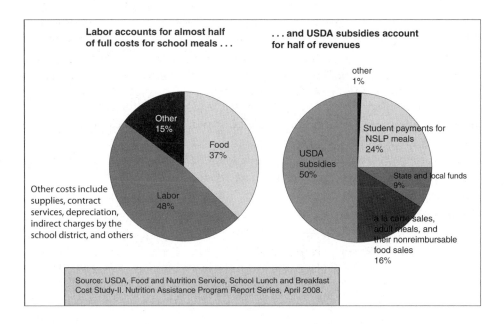

Labor accounts for almost half of full costs for school meals . . .

Other 15%
Food 37%
Labor 48%

Other costs include supplies, contract services, depreciation, indirect charges by the school district, and others

. . . and USDA subsidies account for half of revenues

other 1%
Student payments for NSLP meals 24%
USDA subsidies 50%
State and local funds 9%
a la carte sales, adult meals, and their nonreimbursable food sales 16%

Source: USDA, Food and Nutrition Service, School Lunch and Breakfast Cost Study-II. Nutrition Assistance Program Report Series, April 2008.

According to the case studies, schools have found ways to lower costs and increase revenues. Some SFAs have switched to part-time labor with lower health care benefits, some buy more food in bulk, and some use more ready-to-eat foods. In some cases, SFAs have outsourced meal provision to private foodservice management companies. Schools have joined purchasing cooperatives to reduce food costs, and a small but increasing number of schools are purchasing directly from local farmers. As of May 2008, 1,929 school districts have an operational "farm-to-school" program, according to the National Farm to School network.

Schools have also found creative ways to increase revenues through higher student participation. Most of these strategies have revolved around food preparation changes, lunch scheduling changes, and nutrition education. Smaller efforts have brought students into the process of tasting, selecting, and learning about nutrition through games and parties. Some schools have completely revamped their lunch programs, while others have implemented more gradual changes.

Studies have identified several supporting factors as necessary complements to lunch program changes. First, eliminating or greatly reducing competitive foods has been essential. Students eat more healthful foods and purchase more NSLP meals when their options are reduced. Second, school lunch programs can benefit from buy-in from all stakeholders: superintendents, principals, school foodservice personnel, parents, and students. Efforts to improve nutritional quality have proven successful when everyone is onboard, and particularly when leadership is energetic.

The economics of providing school meals needs to be further investigated, especially in light of recent food and fuel price increases. The 2005–06 FNS cost study is the only study that provides national estimates of the revenues and costs of school lunch operations, and it provides important insights. Contrary to conventional wisdom, the findings suggest that competitive foods are not especially profitable for school food services. Instead, the study suggests that financial solvency is likely to be gained via the most profitable component, the NSLP meals themselves. In FY 2008, 62 percent of public and private school students received or purchased an NSLP meal on an average day, so there is room to expand participation. Serving additional meals raises revenues while spreading the cost of the cafeteria and other fixed costs over more meals.

Another way to increase revenues is for schools to raise the prices charged to students for full and reduced-price NSLP lunches and other foods. According to the SNDA study, in 2004–05, most SFAs charged $1.50 for a full-price NSLP meal and $0.40 for a reduced-price meal. The full price charged to students was significantly lower than the average full cost to produce that meal of $2.91. The gap between prices for paid lunches and full costs helps explain why SFAs with lower rates of free and reduced-price meal participation are vulnerable to deficits.

SFAs historically have been reluctant to raise prices because their main goal as nonprofits is to serve affordable meals. In practical terms, SFAs face the need to balance the increased revenues from a price increase against potential losses from the reduction in meals purchased as a result of the higher price. Little is known of the tradeoffs between higher prices and demand for lunches for most schools.

When schools have needed the significant capital investment to completely overhaul their lunch programs, they have largely turned to their communities for funding. This may be an area where the Federal Government could assist further, as it has in the past when funds were needed to equip school cafeterias.

A clear way to increase revenues relative to costs is to get more students to join the lunch line. Following the lead of successful schools, an important change is to offer freshly made, healthful meals that students help to choose and that they have time to enjoy. Whether this is accomplished by completely revamping the program, by making it more efficient, or by raising prices charged to paying students, schools have shown that providing quality, nutritional meals can be done, and it can lead to higher participation rather than lower.

THE NATIONAL SCHOOL LUNCH PROGRAM FEEDS MORE CHILDREN IN A DAY THAN MCDONALD'S

The NSLP operated in over 101,000 public and nonprofit private schools in 2007. Schools participating in the NSLP served over 5 billion lunches to more than 30 million children in 2007.

Of the 30 million students served in 2007, 15 million students qualified for free lunches, 3 million students paid a reduced price, and 12 million students paid full price. Children from families with incomes below 130 percent of the poverty level are eligible for free meals. Those with incomes between 130 and 185 percent of the poverty level are eligible for reduced-priced meals.

Federal Government contributions to the NSLP were $8.7 billion in 2007, with $7.7 billion in cash payments and $1.04 billion in commodity donations.

NEW IDEAS FROM SCHOOL KITCHENS

Schools have successfully implemented a wide range of changes in their lunch rooms, from dramatic changes to small tweaks. Many have substantially modified their lunch programs by remodeling their kitchens and serving areas and, in some cases, by hiring new foodservice directors. Kitchen renovations can provide needed space for fresh food preparation, storage, and new serving areas, such as salad bars, which are typically popular with students. The Berkeley Unified School District in Berkeley, CA, as part of a public/private partnership called the School Lunch Initiative, has upgraded school kitchens to better handle fresh food and reheat meals made from scratch in a central kitchen. They now have a salad bar in each school; they serve fresh fruits and vegetables daily, and they give priority to locally produced, organic food.

New management can also make a difference. In 2003, Hopkins School District in Minneapolis, MN, hired a new foodservice director with professional foodservice management experience. The initial changes made by the new director were small: Healthy foods were made available as an option and the soda vending machine contract was canceled. After the community approved a bond initiative, more major changes were made: Meals were prepared completely onsite and fresh, low-fat, and whole-grain foods became the only options. Food costs rose, and they charged more for the meal to paying students, but the director was able to keep labor and other non-food costs down to where they had been before the change. Also, students were not allowed to go off campus to buy other food.

Smaller innovations at other schools have included bringing students into the food selection process through tastings and demonstration events. Schools have used marketing-style promotions, games, and parties to highlight different new foods. Wolftrap Elementary in Vienna, VA, sponsors monthly "tasting parties," where students are asked to rate different versions of a healthy entree or snack. Student participation provides the unique perspective that an adult may completely miss, such as whether the food is too messy to eat or whether it can get caught in one's braces. And schools get student buy-in as they move to more nutritious meal options.

Other successful strategies have included changes to the cafeteria environment— longer lunch periods, shorter lunch lines, and pleasant seating areas. Studies have found that, when students have more time to eat and especially when lunch follows recess, they are more likely to eat all of their lunch and thus more likely to eat a balanced meal. Also, when the cafeteria is designed to reduce time in lunch lines, students spend more time eating. Schools have also found that students eat well when there are nice seating areas that are conducive to socializing.

For more information, see *Making It Happen! School Nutrition Success Stories,* FNS-374, USDA, Food and Nutrition Service, U.S. Health and Human Services, Centers for Disease Control and Prevention, and U.S. Department of Education, January 2005.

5

Other Issues:
Housing, Disability, and Early Childhood Education

Editor's Introduction

Each aspect of poverty is interconnected and complex enough to warrant its own section—and, indeed, its own book. Consequently, the final section features articles that touch on housing, disability, and education—three major areas that must be addressed in any nuanced discussion of government policy toward the poor. Each of these topics is explored in relation to overall trends in poverty and social-welfare policies through pairs of articles that present either contrasting or mutually illuminating perspectives.

In "Are Shelters the Answer to Family Homelessness," Ralph da Costa Nunez and Laura M. Caruso describe the dramatic rise in family homelessness that occurred following the boom-and-bust economy in the 1990s, a trend they link directly to the welfare caseload, which dropped 68 percent from 1994 to 2003. The authors also connect the rise in homelessness to a failure to build affordable housing and a lack of jobs that offer both benefits and a living wage. In the second selection, Solomon Moore explores the problems related to the federal government's Section 8 housing voucher program—a public housing alternative that provides tenants with vouchers to relocate to private homes in safer middle-class communities, often in nearby suburbs. Due to the struggling economy, enrollment has skyrocketed in recent years, exacerbating racial and class tensions.

The next two articles address the nation's disability benefit programs—Social Security Disability Benefits (SSD), an entitlement paid for by workers, and Supplemental Security Income (SSI), which provides benefits the poor and/or disabled. Created in 1974 under President Richard Nixon to replace the numerous state-run disability programs that served the same purpose, SSI requires applicants to meet both the federal requirements for physical or mental disability and the limitations on income and resources before they can receive benefits. In the first article, "Disability Cases Last Longer as Backlog Rises," Erik Eckholm points to the main problem with SSD and SSI: a tremendous backlog, due to an increasing number of applicants, funding shortages, and cumbersome processes intended to thwart malingerers. The result, as Eckholm explains, is lengthy waiting periods for needy applicants and an overburdened welfare system. The second selection on disability, "Embracing the Exiles," discusses the effect of the 1996 welfare reform legislation on thousands of political refugees receiving SSI benefits in the United States. The legislation places a seven-year time limit on benefits for immigrants, regardless of refugee status, a period of time that no longer correlates with the lengthy immigration process.

The last two pieces in this chapter address the government's role in early child-care and education programs, focusing on Head Start, a federal program run through the Department of Health and Human Services that provides low income children and their parents with affordable education, health care, sustenance, and other services. In "Starting Right," Joan Lombardi considers what she perceives as the "significant gap between what we know about the earliest years of life and the public policies that support families with infants and toddlers in the United States," suggesting that the government initiatives currently in place are falling short. Finally, in "For Head Start, a Marathon Run," Linda Jacobson and Daniel Sheehan examine the Head Start early childhood education program and recent battles over its funding.

Are Shelters the Answer to Family Homelessness?*

By Ralph da Costa Nunez and Laura M. Caruso
USA Today, January 2003

Family homelessness is undergoing a marked transformation and entering a new stage of unprecedented growth. After shifting from an emergency housing problem in the early 1980s to one of sustained poverty during the 1990s, homelessness is on the verge of taking yet another turn. Limitations on the availability of public assistance and a booming, then faltering, economy have destabilized millions of families and ultimately forced thousands into homelessness.

Twenty years ago, one-time housing emergencies—fires, hazardous living conditions, and personal calamities—were the primary cause of family homelessness. Forced out of their homes, families required short-term emergency shelter until they were able to locate new housing. Because of the Reagan Administration's reductions in housing subsidies and social service programs, followed by the welfare reforms of the 1990s, homelessness grew tremendously, taking on an entirely new dimension. On average, homeless families are substantially younger, less educated, and poorer than those of the 1980s. In essence, an entire generation has been notched down into a chronic poverty that claims homelessness as one of its most defining characteristics.

For many, homelessness is not simply a housing issue. Rather, it stems from poor education, lack of employable skills, inadequate health care, domestic violence, child abuse, foster care, and insufficient child care. Many of today's homeless families are headed by a young unmarried mother, with two or three children. She grew up in poverty, may have experienced domestic violence, and never completed high school, often dropping out due to pregnancy. She has at least one child suffering from a chronic health problem and has had trouble enrolling her kids in school. She has lived with a relative or partner, or doubled-up prior to becoming homeless, and left her last residence due to overcrowding, a disagreement, or violence. She currently is unemployed due to a lack of work skills or child care—or both—and is dependent on public assistance to support herself and her family.

As for the children, homelessness is usually not a brief or singular experience—27% have been homeless more than once, living in at least three different residences in a single year. Without permanent housing, such youngsters endure frequent moves—at a rate 16 times that of the typical American family—from motels to doubled-up apartments with family or friends to shelters. On average, they are homeless 10 months at a time, or an entire school year, a period fraught with educational and emotional setbacks. Nationally, 20% repeat a grade in school and 16% are enrolled in special education classes—rates 100% and 33%, respectively, higher than their nonhomeless peers. More than half change schools once a year, and over one-third switch two or more times, setting them back at least six months each time.

Today in America, over 600,000 families [and] more than 1,000,000 children are homeless, living in shelters, on the streets, in cars, and on campgrounds. According to the U.S. Conference of Mayors, requests for emergency shelter by families increased an average of 22% in 2001 and 17% the year before. After 20 years of steady increases and with additional changes in welfare reform again on the table, why shouldn't we expect more of the same? Isn't it time to move in a new direction? First, though, it is necessary to understand the primary factors that have contributed to this dramatic rise—a shortage of affordable housing, a decrease in jobs paying a living wage, and welfare reform. What these trends reveal is a new era of homelessness dominated by a growing class of Americans living for long periods in shelters.

Over the last three decades, the stock of affordable housing has declined significantly, so that, by 1995, the gap between low-income renters and low-cost rental units, nonexistent in 1970, widened to more than 4,400,000. From 1996 to 1998, the most-recent data available, the situation worsened as the number of affordable units further decreased by 19%, or 1,300,000 units, due to the demolition of distressed properties and a shift of privately owned subsidized units to open-rental market rates.

In response to these trends, more families are forced to pay a larger share of their income in rent. In the last 20 years, the proportion of households with children paying more than 30% of their income on housing rose from 15 to 28%—a burden that the Federal government reports places low-income families at risk of homelessness. Today, 6,000,000 households, with over 4,000,000 children, have worst-case housing needs, earning less than 50% of the local median income and either paying more than half of their income in rent, living in severely substandard housing, or both. As a result, millions of children and their families are living on the brink of homelessness with no alternative.

Also contributing to the housing crisis and to homelessness is the decreasing value of wages. From 1979 to 1999, the most-recent data available, hourly salary for low-wage workers fell nine percent, adjusted for inflation—the result of a shift away from higher-paying manufacturing jobs to lower-paying service positions. These are typically very-low-wage or part-time jobs with few or no benefits, leaving employees with minimal resources to care for their families. For example, in

2000, a full-time worker earning minimum wage could not afford the fair-market rent for a two-bedroom apartment anywhere in the U.S. Instead, his or her family is first forced into a doubled-up living situation, then ultimately to a shelter.

This economic shift is particularly sobering in light of recent and upcoming welfare policy changes. More than 9,000,000 people (two-thirds of them children) have left the welfare rolls since 1994—a 68% reduction in caseloads. As families leave public assistance, they are forced into a competitive low-wage market. A Center on Budget and Policy Priorities report found that those who find jobs after welfare typically earn between $8,000 and $10,800 annually—well below the poverty line of $14,129 for a family of three. Considering the average fair-market rents, those leaving public assistance could end up paying between 50 and 75% of their income on housing.

Moreover, welfare reductions have directly fueled homelessness. In a study of 22 cities, 37% of families had their welfare benefits reduced or cut in the last year, with 20% becoming homeless as a result. Most strikingly, in Philadelphia and Seattle, more than 50% had their benefits reduced or cut and, among those, 42 and 38%, respectively, became homeless as a result. A second study of six states found that, within six months of families losing their welfare benefits, 25% doubled-up on housing to save money and 23% moved because they could not afford rent. In San Diego County, welfare reform not only resulted in homelessness, but in disintegrated families, as 18% of those parents whose benefits were reduced or cut lost a child to foster care. With the full impact of time limits yet to come, the ongoing effects of welfare reform highlight the changing state of homelessness.

More and more families are seeking subsidized housing at a time following 20 years of reduced Federal support. In 1986, for the first time ever, Federal outlays for housing assistance fell more than 50%, from $80,000,000 to $38,000,000, never again achieving an adequate level of support. In 1995, the number of Federally assisted households fell and no new units of assistance were funded for four years. As a result, lengthy waiting lists for Section 8 housing, a Federal program that gives incentives to landlords to provide low-income housing and rent subsidies as well as for public housing, are now the norm. Between 1998 and 1999 alone, the most-recent data available, Section 8 waiting lists increased by 34%. In Los Angeles and Newark, N.J., the wait for Section 8 is 10 years, and 52% of all homeless families in America are on subsidized housing waiting lists.

Clearly, the stage has been set for yet another generation of homeless families. While we continue to demand the development of new affordable housing, it is not on the horizon, and for many families, housing alone is not sufficient. Those who have worked closely with homeless families know that many need supportive services in order to maintain their own home, hold a job, and live independently. So, why not offer supportive housing with services? Government is not building significant levels of low-income housing and, whether intentional or not, has spent billions of dollars over many years erecting a massive shelter system across America. These shelters have become homes to over 1,000,000 kids and their families. Without alternatives, the homeless find themselves turning to shelters as the one remaining element of a dwindling safety net, often as a last resort to keep their families together. Yet, it is here—in shelters—that the reduction of family homelessness may actually begin.

Shelters and transitional housing themselves may be the catalyst for reducing homelessness by providing on-site services and programs that address the root causes of this new poverty. By using the national shelter infrastructure already in place to provide immediate housing—given the history of paltry housing options in the face of an economic boom and especially in light of a new national focus on homeland security—we can enhance services to be comprehensive and focused on building long-term skills that foster independence and economic viability. If we take the emergency out of the situation and allow them to focus on building real skills and work histories, we offer families their first step on a path to self-determination.

Fifteen years ago, shelters were stark, temporary, scary places, as families lived in congregate settings, on cots huddled together in an open space. They were gymnasiums, armories, and church basements—none an appropriate place to call home. However, many of today's shelters are different. They have private rooms with cooking facilities; some are apartments with one or two bedrooms, which are safe, clean, and offer a multitude of services. In fact, these shelters are becoming surrogate communities, places from which parents commute to work and children go to school. (Twenty-six percent of families in shelters are currently employed.) Many provide child care and after-school programs for youngsters, and job-readiness training and life skills for adults. They are places where parents are raising their families and that have become home to those who live there.

In a shelter-turned-community, directors should advocate for resources for their residents just like elected officials do for their constituents, and staff must link families to a variety of educational and employment options just like guidance counselors do for their students. For homeless families, a stay in the shelter community could be a second chance to advance literacy levels, finish high school, build a work history, and enhance life skills, and this is only the beginning. They can be expanded and financed through housing assistance vouchers targeted to them; residents who work could pay some rent; and partnerships with the public and private sectors could further enrich services. The more comprehensive the network of shelter-based services, the more vibrant and effective this community becomes.

The acceptance and expansion of such a plan—putting shelter communities to work to reduce family homelessness—requires bold leadership and vision. Yet, it can be done, and, in many instances, the process has already begun. A real and meaningful plan to end family homelessness in this country must begin by being politically honest with the American people. Government has not and, in all likelihood, will not be producing low-income housing on any acceptable level in the near future. Instead, we are going to have to acknowledge that, for the time being, a shelter is indeed a home, and one that must continue to evolve into a community with opportunities.

As Program Moves Poor to Suburbs, Tensions Follow[*]

By Solomon Moore
The New York Times, August 8, 2008

From the tough streets of Oakland, where so many of Alice Payne's relatives and friends had been shot to death, the newspaper advertisement for a federally assisted rental property in this Northern California suburb was like a bridge across the River Jordan.

Ms. Payne, a 42-year-old African-American mother of five, moved to Antioch in 2006. With the local real estate market slowing and a housing voucher covering two-thirds of the rent, she found she could afford a large, new home, with a pool, for $2,200 a month.

But old problems persisted. When her estranged husband was arrested, the local housing authority tried to cut off her subsidy, citing disturbances at her house. Then the police threatened to prosecute her landlord for any criminal activity or public nuisances caused by the family. The landlord forced the Paynes to leave when their lease was up.

Under the Section 8 federal housing voucher program, thousands of poor, urban and often African-American residents have left hardscrabble neighborhoods in the nation's largest cities and resettled in the suburbs.

Law enforcement experts and housing researchers argue that rising crime rates follow Section 8 recipients to their new homes, while other experts discount any direct link. But there is little doubt that cultural shock waves have followed the migration. Social and racial tensions between newcomers and their neighbors have increased, forcing suburban communities like Antioch to re-evaluate their civic identities along with their methods of dealing with the new residents.

The foreclosure crisis gnawing away at overbuilt suburbs has accelerated that migration, and the problems. Antioch is one of many suburbs in the midst of a full-blown mortgage meltdown that has seen property owners seeking out low-income renters to fill vacant homes. The most recent Contra Costa County records available show that from 2003 to 2005, the number of Section 8 households in Antioch grew by 50 percent, to about 1,500 from 1,000. Many new residents are African-American; Antioch's black population has grown to about 20 percent, from 3 percent in 1990.

Federally assisted tenants in Antioch brought a class action lawsuit against the police department last month, claiming racial discrimination, intimidation and illegal property searches. The lawsuit, which was filed in the Northern District of California, claims that the police routinely questioned Section 8 residents about their housing status and wrote letters to the county's housing authority recommending termination of subsidies. They say the police also threatened Section 8 landlords for infractions by tenants. A December 2007 study of Antioch police records by Public Advocates, a law firm in San Francisco, counted 67 investigations of black households, compared with 59 of white families; black households, it found, are four times as likely to be searched based on noncriminal complaints and to be contacted by the police in the first place.

Chief James Hyde of the Antioch Police Department denied that his officers routinely asked whether tenants were Section 8 recipients and said that the police department did not have information about which homes were on federal assistance. But Chief Hyde also said that the local housing authority was not meeting its obligation to screen tenants properly, and that as his department focused on nuisance issues, the police had become a de facto enforcement arm of the federal government.

"Other cities have come asking us for guidance," Chief Hyde said.

The Section 8 program is designed to encourage low-income tenants to settle in middle-income areas by subsidizing 60 percent of their rent. The United States Department of Housing and Urban Development issued 50,000 more vouchers for suburban relocations in 2007 than in 2005, bringing the total number of renter families to 2.1 million.

Federal officials and housing experts say that the increase in vouchers was offset by people being forced out of federal housing projects that closed and by renters moving into foreclosed properties. According to the National Low Income Housing Coalition, a nonprofit advocacy and research group, 30 percent to 40 percent of residents in foreclosed properties were renters, many of whom have since sought federal assistance.

Linda Couch, the coalition's deputy director, said families often waited a decade or more for housing vouchers.

Demand for subsidized suburban housing, meanwhile, is outstripping supply. In Salinas, Calif., applicants circled an entire block around a housing authority office earlier this month. Mobile, Ala., has 3,400 Section 8 families, and 2,000 more awaiting homes.

Sociologists have long claimed that leaving behind high-crime, low-employment neighborhoods for the middle-class suburbs buoys the fortunes of impoverished tenants. An article in the July/August edition of *The Atlantic Monthly*, however, cited findings by researchers at the University of Memphis that crime in Memphis appeared to migrate with voucher recipients. More broadly, a 2006 Georgia Institute of Technology study found that every time a neighborhood experienced three foreclosures per 100 owner-occupied properties in a year, violent crime increased by approximately 7 percent.

As Antioch's population grew to 101,000 in 2005, from 73,386 in 1995, the city built about 4,000 housing units in the early years of this decade.

Now it has one of the highest foreclosure rates in the state, with about 23 of every 1,000 homeowners losing their homes as of June, according to DataQuick, a real estate information clearinghouse.

While total crime in Antioch declined by 15 percent in the first three months of this year, compared to the same period in 2007, violent crime increased by about 16 percent, according to city statistics. Robberies and assaults accounted for most of that rise.

In an incident report filed with the Antioch Police Department, Natalie and Darin Rouse complained of constant problems with gang members' blaring car stereos and under-age drinking on the street. In a written account, they blamed "gross community overdevelopment, affirmative action loopholes and incompetent state government management of federal affordable housing programs" for the problems.

Several white women, all professionals who attend the same church and have lived in Antioch for 12 years or more, recently sat outside a Starbucks coffee shop and discussed how their declining home equity had trapped them in a city they no longer recognize.

"My father got held up at gunpoint while he was renting a car to a young African-American man," said Rebecca Gustafson, 35, who owns a graphics and Web design company with her husband. Ms. Gustafson said her car had also been broken into three times before being stolen from her driveway.

Laura Reynolds, 36, an emergency room nurse, said that she often came home to her Country Hills development tract after working a late-shift to find young black teenagers strolling through her neighborhood.

"I know it sounds horrible, but they're scary. I'm sorry," said Ms. Reynolds, who like her two friends said she was conflicted about her newfound fear of black youths. "Sometimes I question myself, and I think, 'Would I feel this way if they were Mexican or white?'"

Housing advocates argue that the impact of Section 8 in Antioch and other communities is exaggerated and that Section 8 houses make up only a small amount of the real estate market. Section 8 homes rarely exceed more than 2 percent of available housing in any metropolitan area; in Antioch the average is 8 percent, according to housing officials.

Brad Seligman, a lawyer with the Impact Fund, a nonprofit civil rights advocacy group based in San Francisco that is representing Section 8 tenants in Antioch, along with groups like the American Civil Liberties Union and Public Advocates, accused the city's police department of racially profiling black subsidized tenants. The N.A.A.C.P. has made similar accusations.

"Instead of driving while black, it's renting while black," Mr. Seligman said.

Thomas and Karen Coleman and their three children were the only black family on their street when they moved to Antioch in 2003 with a housing voucher.

In June 2007, a neighbor told the police that Mr. Coleman had threatened him. Officers from the police community action team visited the house and demanded to be allowed in.

"I cracked the door open, but they pushed me out of the way," Ms. Coleman said.

The officers searched the house even though they did not have a warrant, said the Colemans, who are now part of the class-action suit against the department. The police questioned Mr. Coleman, a parolee at the time, about his living arrangement. He explained that he and his wife were separated but in the process of reconciling. The police accused the family of violating a Section 8 rule that only listed tenants can live in a subsidized home.

After the raid, officers made repeated visits to the Coleman home and to Mr. Coleman's job at a movie theater. They also sent a letter to the county housing department recommending that the Colemans be removed from federal housing assistance, a recommendation the authority rejected.

"They kept harassing me until I was off parole," Mr. Coleman said.

Disability Cases Last Longer as Backlog Rises[*]

By Erik Eckholm
The New York Times, December 10, 2007

Steadily lengthening delays in the resolution of Social Security disability claims have left hundreds of thousands of people in a kind of purgatory, now waiting as long as three years for a decision.

Two-thirds of those who appeal an initial rejection eventually win their cases.

But in the meantime, more and more people have lost their homes, declared bankruptcy or even died while awaiting an appeals hearing, say lawyers representing claimants and officials of the Social Security Administration, which administers disability benefits for those judged unable to work or who face terminal illness.

The agency's new plan to hire at least 150 new appeals judges to whittle down the backlog, which has soared to 755,000 from 311,000 in 2000, will require $100 million more than the president requested this year and still more in the future. The plan has been delayed by the standoff between Congress and the White House over domestic appropriations.

There are 1,025 judges currently at work, and the wait for an appeals hearing averages more than 500 days, compared with 258 in 2000. Without new hirings, federal officials predict even longer waits and more of the personal tragedies that can result from years of painful uncertainty.

Progress against the backlog, if it happens, cannot undo the three years that Belinda Virgil of Fayetteville, N.C., has worried about her future since her initial application was turned down.

Tethered to an oxygen tank 24 hours a day because of emphysema and life-threatening sleep apnea, Ms. Virgil lost her apartment and has alternated between a sofa in her daughter's crowded house and a friend's place as she waits for an answer to her appeal.

"It's been hell," said Ms. Virgil, 44, who finally got her hearing in November and is awaiting the outcome. "I've got no money for Christmas, I move from house to house, and I'm getting really depressed."

The disability process is complex, and the standard for approval has, from the inception of the program in the 1950s, been intentionally strict to prevent malingering and drains on the treasury. But it is also inevitably subjective in some cases, like those involving mental illness or pain that cannot be tested.

In a standard tougher than those of most private plans, recipients must prove that because of physical or mental disabilities they are unable to do "any kind of substantial work" for at least 12 months—if an engineer could not do his job but could work as a clerk, he would not qualify—or prove that an illness is expected "to result in death."

In a recent interview, the commissioner of Social Security, Michael J. Astrue, said that outright fraud was rare but that many cases on appeal were borderline. In addition, widely publicized charges in the 1970s that money had been wasted on recipients whose conditions improved led to tighter scrutiny.

Of the roughly 2.5 million disability applicants each year now, about two-thirds are turned down initially by state agencies, which make decisions with federal oversight based on paper records but no face-to-face interview. Most of those who are refused give up at that point or after a failed request for local reconsideration.

But of the more than 575,000 who go on to file appeals—putting them in the vast line for a hearing before a special federal judge—two-thirds eventually win a reversal.

Mr. Astrue and other officials attribute the high number of reversals to several causes. Those who file appeals tend to be those with stronger cases and lawyers who help them gather persuasive medical data. During the extended waiting period, a person's condition may worsen, strengthening the case. The judges see applicants in person and have more discretion to grant benefits in borderline cases.

Requiring face-to-face interviews at the initial stage could reduce the number of appeals, Mr. Astrue said, "but given the huge volume of cases coming through, it would be incredibly costly, and the Congress is not willing to fund that."

The growing delays in the appeal process over the last decade resulted in part from litigation and financing shortages that prevented the hiring of new administrative law judges. In addition, the number of applications is rising as baby boomers reach their 50s and 60s.

"Once the system got overloaded, it fell farther and farther behind," said Rick Warsinskey, legislative director of the National Council of Social Security Management Associations, which represents managers from the agency.

If approved, those who have paid into Social Security receive income comparable to retirement benefits, averaging more than $1,000 a month and potentially more. The poor, and severely disabled children, receive Supplemental Security Income checks that will be $637 a month in 2008.

Charles T. Hall's law firm in Raleigh has the state's largest disability practice, with six lawyers representing some 2,500 clients, usually working on contingency and collecting 25 percent of back payments, to a limit of $5,300. Mr. Hall said that about one client a month died while awaiting a hearing. Far more clients, he said, run out of money and are evicted from rental units or lose their homes.

In the past, said Walter Patterson, a disability lawyer in Statesville, N.C., clients who received a foreclosure warning were pushed up the waiting list for quicker hearings. But as the hearing offices have become overwhelmed, he said, they now expedite cases only after seeing an actual eviction notice—usually too late to help.

Thomas Airington, 48, who formerly ran a car-emissions testing business, was told his appeal, filed last spring, would be expedited when he showed officials an eviction notice. In the meantime he lost the house, which his parents had bequeathed him. A hearing date has still not been set.

"If I'd been approved in time, I could have saved my house," said Mr. Airington, who is staying with a brother near Raleigh.

Mr. Airington has pins in his spine from a car accident in 1992, shattered a knee when he fell 30 feet in 2005, has nerve damage in his feet and chronic arthritis and depression. The rejection letter he is appealing said, "We have determined that the condition is not severe enough to preclude work."

Mr. Airington said he tried a desk job but found he could not sit for long, and tried working as a stocker in a grocery store but could not reach for shelves. Whatever the outcome, he, like many applicants, is in limbo while he waits.

The extended delays can also mean extra burdens for state welfare agencies. In New York State, about half the 38,000 people now waiting on disability appeals, for an average of 21 months, are receiving cash assistance from the state, said Michael Hayes, spokesman for the Office of Temporary and Disability Assistance.

Mr. Astrue, the latest of several Social Security commissioners to promise speedier decisions, said the agency had already taken steps to ensure quicker initial approval for those most clearly eligible and was holding more hearings by video.

But by all accounts, a major increase in money, judges and support staff will be needed to have a significant impact.

Mr. Astrue said that if the budget impasse continued for too long, leaving the agency budget at its current level, "not only will we not do any hiring, we're looking at furloughs."

A first step of raising the number of judges to 1,200 will require at least $100 million extra for the agency beyond the $9.6 billion that President Bush has proposed for the 2008 fiscal year, Mr. Astrue said. Within a wide-ranging, $151 billion health, education and labor bill passed in November, the Democratic-controlled Congress voted for a $275 million increase for the agency. But Mr. Bush vetoed the bill, calling it profligate.

If the stalemate continues, the government will probably operate on the basis of continuing resolutions, which will keep agency spending at last year's level and doom the plan to add judges.

Richard and Vicki Wild and their adult son Mark, of Hillsborough, N.C., were mystified that Mark's case would ever require a judge.

Hospitalized with increasing frequency since his severe diabetes was discovered at age 19, when he was found unconscious in a bus station, Mark Wild was eager to work as a chef. But over 15 years, he tried and lost jobs as a waiter and a cook. He had to drop out of culinary school because he was hospitalized so often, his parents said.

"We had 10 years' worth of hospital records and unanimous opinions from the doctors," said Richard Wild, 62, who until recently was a computer analyst. But his son's initial application was turned down in 2003.

The family had sunk into debt because of medical bills, nearly losing their house of 30 years, but found a lawyer to file an appeal. The son, by then in his mid-30s, had to wait two more years to get a hearing scheduled, with no income and little life outside his parents' home and the hospital.

As his hearing date in October 2006 approached, Mark Wild told his parents that he feared another rejection. "It was his last chance at any dignity, and he said if they turned him down it would be too much to take," recalled Mrs. Wild, a nurse.

On Tuesday, Oct. 17, 2006, just a few days before the hearing, Mrs. Wild woke up to find her son gone. On his desk lay his watch, his ring and a bullet.

On that Thursday, Mrs. Wild, 55, got a call at work from their lawyer. "I just wanted to give you the good news," she said he told her. "Somehow the judge has already approved the disability, it's a done deal, Mark's got it."

Two hours later, a deputy sheriff and a chaplain arrived to say that hunters had found Mark Wild's body in the woods, dead of a self-inflicted gunshot wound.

"No one can say for sure, but we're convinced that his despondency and fear about the disability decision contributed to his death," said Mrs. Wild, who wears a pinch of her son's ashes in a small tube on a necklace.

Mr. Wild has tried to go back to work, but says he is so depressed he cannot do his job. He is applying for disability, but knows that he cannot expect an answer anytime soon.

Embracing the Exiles[*]

The Forward, October 20, 2006

Disabled and elderly refugees are being left in the lurch by a misguided law.

Shmuel Kaplan, an 80-year-old amputee, breathed a sigh of relief in 1997 when the United States granted him political asylum after he fled antisemitism in the former Soviet Union. Two years later, we similarly received an Iranian boy, Rouzbeh Aliaghaei, and his parents. His mother was a high school teacher who had been imprisoned and twice fired for decrying the treatment of women and their lack of freedom. Nine-year-old Rouzbeh understood little about his family's flight—he is afflicted with a rare genetic disorder resulting in profound mental retardation.

Ever lifting the lamp of freedom beside the golden door, in poet Emma Lazarus's famous phrase, America welcomed these immigrants on humanitarian grounds, fulfilling our obligation to provide safe harbor to victims of persecution. Because of their severe disabilities, the impoverished Shmuel and Rouzbeh qualified for Medicaid health insurance and the special support of $603 a month through Supplemental Security Income (SSI), the same safety net available to permanently disabled American citizens at the poverty level.

But now Shmuel and Rouzbeh are in crisis: Their SSI has been yanked away. Still unable to support themselves, they have hit the end of a seven-year SSI time limit. In an unprecedented departure from federal policies toward refugees, as part of the 1996 welfare reform law the federal government restricted SSI benefits to refugees to their first seven years in the country.

This policy has proved to be disastrous for Shmuel, Rouzbeh and thousands like them, for a variety of reasons. Established in the pre-9/11 era, the cut-off limit was based on the assumption that seven years was ample time for refugees receiving SSI to become citizens, and thus able to continue receiving SSI benefits. The 1996 law also mandated that all other newly arriving legal immigrants eligible for SSI as elderly or disabled would be restricted access to it until they became American citizens.

In retrospect, the 1996 legislation has yielded unexpected results in the post-9/11 era. To naturalize, one must first obtain permanent resident status. Rouzbeh's parents, for example, applied at the earliest time possible; nevertheless, it took five years for them to receive their green cards, granting them status as legal permanent residents. The naturalization process then necessitates the refugee to exhaust a five-year permanent residence requirement.

Thereafter, even the most determined applicant faces further processing delays—there is now a backlog of almost one million naturalization applications at the U.S. Citizenship and Immigration Services agency, primarily due to name and security checks. For Shmuel and Rouzbeh, as with many other disabled and elderly refugees, their mental impairments and age present further obstacles to naturalization. Six thousand refugees already have been terminated from SSI. If federal law is not adjusted to present realities, 40,000 more terminations are projected.

Linking SSI eligibility to citizenship for disabled refugees is fundamentally flawed. A bipartisan U.S. Commission on Immigration Reform recommended against its linkage as a debasement of citizenship, reasoning that we should not make deprivation the incentive to naturalize. As well, long-standing federal immigration policy recognizes that refugees often must escape with no assets and no relatives here to support them. As a consequence, our laws have long exempted refugees in contrast to other potential immigrants from exclusion on public charge grounds and from requirements that they have affidavits of support from legally responsible sponsors.

Refugees affected by the cut-off include Russian Jews who were persecuted for their religion, Catholics fleeing violence in Indonesia, Iraqi Kurds who escaped Saddam Hussein's wrath, Cubans who fled the Castro regime and Hmong who fought on the side of the United States during the Vietnam War. Most refugees in the United States are employed and self-sufficient. A minority of refugees, however, suffer disabling physical and mental impairments. Like American citizens, they need the assistance of SSI and Medicaid to sustain their lives.

An extension of SSI is supported in principle by the White House as well as by a bipartisan group of legislators sponsoring bills in the Senate and House (S. 667 and H.R. 899). Yet these measures have not been treated as priorities. They need to be passed this year before Congress adjourns for the year. And even better, Congress should enact legislation that would provide full access to SSI for disabled refugees.

The Mother of Exiles is Emma Lazarus's metaphor for the Statue of Liberty and, by extension, the United States itself. The phrase embodies the long-standing ideal of our nation to embrace the tempest-tossed. As a compassionate country, America should not be terminating SSI for its disabled and aged refugees.

Starting Right*

Building on Proven Strategies to Promote Development in Very Young Children

By Joan Lombardi
American Prospect, November 2004

In the mid-1990s, newsstands across the country brimmed with magazines touting new research on brain development, and the "science" of early-childhood development was championed from the East Room to the hearing room, from the boardroom to the living room. Yet almost a decade later, there is still a significant gap between what we know about the earliest years of life and the public policies that support families with infants and toddlers in the United States.

Why the gap? There is no simple answer; rather a combination of factors has left this country without a coherent family policy—and lagging far behind virtually all other advanced nations when it comes to support for families with children under age 3. Perhaps the strongest influence has been the cultural tradition that considers the care of very young children the sole responsibility of their parents. Any attempts to develop policies that are perceived as "interfering" with this responsibility have been taboo. Even a policy to give parents time off during the critical first year of a baby's life has been stubbornly hard to win.

Yet the sense that parents must "go it alone" is not the only thing that stands in the way of change. Traditional thinking on education still has not fully embraced the concept that children are "born learning," despite compelling evidence from the newest brain research. Similarly, our policies do not fully reflect what science teaches about the vitally important contribution of parents and caregivers to a child's education. Education reform has focused much more on what goes on inside the school building and much less on what goes on at home and in the community.

Strategies to promote the healthy development of and early education for our youngest children—starting well before school age—should be the next frontier of education reform. We need a more cohesive set of policies that can support the earliest forms of education while respecting the range of choices parents make for their families. Along with access to prenatal and early health care, such policies would address parental leave and preparation for parenthood for all families; improved child care for working families; and access to comprehensive early-childhood services for expectant parents, babies, and toddlers at greatest risk.

It is widely recognized that parents need time and support to be with their newborn baby to establish the strong early bonds that lead to positive and healthy relationships. Indeed, while most industrialized countries guarantee paid parental leave, the United States is not among them. The closest we've come to a national response—the Family and Medical Leave Act of 1993—provides 12 weeks of unpaid leave and covers only about 60 percent of private-sector employees, and only about 45 percent are both covered and eligible.

Predictably, low-income working families are least likely to benefit because they can rarely afford to take unpaid leave, have jobs with the least flexibility, and have the hardest time finding quality infant care and reliable transportation. Welfare reform in the 1990s only compounded the problem, allowing states to require women with children under age 1 to participate in work activities, while funding for child care in the past few years has failed to keep up with demand.

In recent years, advocates for family and medical leave have turned to the states. In 2002, California became the first state in the nation to enact paid family leave, expanding the state disability insurance program to provide up to six weeks of partial wage-replacement benefits to workers who take time off to care for a new baby or seriously ill family member. According to the National Partnership for Women and Families, five states (and Puerto Rico) have state-administered Temporary Disability Insurance systems (or require employers to offer them). Such systems provide partial wage replacement to employees who are temporarily disabled for medical reasons, including pregnancy or birth-related medical reasons. Efforts to enact paid leave have been introduced in more than two dozen states.

One innovative solution, the At-Home Infant Care (AHIC) program, was pioneered by Minnesota and Montana in response to the lack of good infant care. AHIC gives low-income families a partial subsidy so they can remain home to care for their very young children. Minnesota families could participate if they were eligible for child-care assistance and had children under age 1. In Montana, eligibility was set at 150 percent of poverty for families with children under age 2. Parents reported both developmental and financial benefits. Despite the promise and interest in this model, though, tight budgets have hampered its progress.

Most children under age 3 have working parents. It is well-established that the quality of the infant and toddler care on which millions of these parents depend each day can affect a child's well-being. Despite this knowledge, affordable, high-quality care remains out of reach for many working parents—particularly low-income ones, whose children could benefit most from the enrichment a good program might provide. Families with very young children have the fewest child-care options and pay the highest price for care. Quality is stretched thin due to low wages, high turnover, and limited training opportunities for providers. Child-care resource and referral agencies across the country receive more calls from parents seeking affordable, quality infant care than any other type of child care. Even when child-care assistance is available, it most often does not cover the full cost of quality care.

In an effort to address this national need, Congress has appropriated an additional $100 million each year since 1998 to improve the quality of infant care through the nation's main child-care program, the Child Care and Development Block Grant (CCDBG). With these funds, states have been launching new strategies, creating innovative training and credentialing for infant- and toddler-care providers, expanding family child-care networks, and developing supports for "family, friends and neighbor care"—the type most often used by parents of very young children and by low-income families. While all these efforts are important, they are only initial steps forward; much more is needed to make high-quality infant care the national priority it deserves to be.

The early head start program was designed with this challenge in mind. Added to the Head Start program in 1994, it was designed to offer comprehensive health, family-support, and education services to expectant parents and infants and toddlers living in poverty. In fiscal year 2003, Early Head Start served nearly 62,000 children under age 3 in more than 650 programs across the country. Services are delivered through home visits, center-based programs, or a combination of the two.

So far, the results have been promising. A rigorous evaluation of Early Head Start has shown positive impacts on children's cognitive, language, and social-emotional development—and, importantly, solid effects on their parents, too. Results were stronger when programs started during pregnancy and when standards were carefully implemented.

As is too often the case, though, too few are helped: Early Head Start still serves only 3 percent of the more than 2 million poor children under age 3 nationwide. And with poverty among very young children growing, expansion of services to infants and toddlers is more important than ever. With more and more states investing in preschool programs, the logical next step for Head Start is to expand downward. Because we know that most children enter the program already behind in language development and other skills important for school readiness, we simply can't afford to wait to start them on the right road.

There are more than 11 million infants and toddlers living in the United States. If we are indeed committed to making top-notch education a priority, it must start well before they reach the preschool door. And it must bridge partisan and ideological differences that have impeded progress for far too long. The next Congress and administration can start by expanding the Family and Medical Leave Act to provide benefits to more families, and by providing incentives to states to experiment with paid leave and programs like the At-Home Infant Care model. Reauthorization of both Head Start and the CCDBG provide important opportunities for change, too. The funding set aside for infants and toddlers in the CCDBG should be authorized and expanded, and each state should be required to have a plan to ensure better care for babies and toddlers. Head Start programs across the country should be allowed to serve expectant parents and children under age 3 if that is what their communities need.

These steps can lay the foundation of a compassionate agenda, can lead to long-term benefits, and are the most basic elements of a comprehensive approach to education reform—a goal that everyone can embrace.

For Head Start, A Marathon Run[*]

By Linda Jacobson and Daniel Sheehan
Education Week, April 25, 2007

Sitting around small tables, the 3- and 4-year-olds scooped oatmeal into plastic foam bowls and poured milk from pitchers into paper cups, without spilling.

"You know, Hector, you don't have to eat it, but why don't you just try it?" urged Michele Gonzalez, an associate teacher in a Head Start classroom here on the campus of Valencia Elementary School, east of Los Angeles.

As the children nibbled on pear slices, Ms. Gonzalez got them to talk about the classroom materials they wanted to use during "work time." Some headed for the housekeeping area, others set up farm sets with plastic animals, and a few sat on the floor listening to songs about colors while they followed along in large books.

Meanwhile, in a back office, parents gathered for a monthly meeting after dropping off their children. The nutritional, social, and educational needs of disadvantaged children—combined with opportunities for parents to be involved—have been elements of the Head Start program since it started more than 40 years ago as part of President Lyndon B. Johnson's War on Poverty.

"For disadvantaged folks, the comprehensive services have always been the flagship" of the federal child-development program," said Channel Wilkins, the director of the Office of Head Start, part of the federal government's Administration for Children and Families.

But as federal debate over reauthorization of the program drags on for a fourth year, Head Start finds itself coping with pressures that its founders might not have anticipated.

In some locations around the country, Head Start grantees that have served communities for decades have been forced to promote their services or risk losing children to state-funded programs that have become increasingly popular.

Supporters of Head Start, which has a budget of about $6.8 billion for the current fiscal year, also say they have had to endure flat funding in recent years.

The program's adaptability is evident here at the Valencia site, which is run by Options, a private, nonprofit child-care and human-services agency based in nearby West Covina.

Next to the portable building housing the Head Start class are two more classrooms called Child Start—a collaboration involving federal Head Start money and state child-care funding that allows low-income working parents to have full-day, year-round care for their preschoolers.

The partnership with the California Department of Education—like similar arrangements throughout the country—shows how "a national program with local roots," as Mr. Wilkins calls it, can retain its identity, but still accommodate the needs of parents" and an ever-expanding landscape of early-childhood-education programs.

"In 1965, they were the only kid on the block," said W. Steven Barnett, the director of the National Institute for Early Education Eesearch; based at Rutgers University in New Brunswick, N. J. "In 2005, that's just not true."

COMPETING PRESSURES

From the standpoint of the National Head Start Association, the Alexandria, Va.-based group that represents Head Start's employees and families, the program has been on the defensive over the past several years.

Supporters say Head Start had to fight against what they labeled as an effort by the Bush administration to "dismantle" the program—first by moving it to the Department of Education from the Department of Health and Human Services and second, by funding the program through block grants on a pilot basis for a handful of states.

Sarah Greene, the president of the National Head Start Association, said the intense spotlight on the program started early this decade, in part with some Republican members of Congress highlighting the fiscal troubles of certain grantees, leaving the public with the impression that mismanagement was widespread.

"Those were vicious attacks," Ms. Greene said. "But we're like any other agency. There are always a few people not doing their jobs the way they should."

John Bancroft, the executive director of Head Start at the Puget Sound Educational Service District in Washington state, which serves suburban Seattle and suburban Tacoma, said President Bush's then-new administration was trying to "put its stamp on the program," maybe without realizing how negatively those proposals would be received by the Head Start community.

As the reauthorization process moves forward, Mr. Bancroft said he sees bipartisan cooperation on the Senate and House versions of the bills—both of which include a provision that would drop the National Reporting System, a controversial package of tests administered to 4- and 5-year-olds twice a year.

"It has been quite a distraction," Mr. Bancroft said about the testing system, adding that on top of pre-existing assessments his program has used, the "NES has been no use to us."

But Mr. Wilkins said the test has been useful in determining how to design technical assistance. For example, past NRS results showed that children in the program needed stronger early-math skills, and so more attention has been focused on that area, he said. Last fall, the test also was expanded to include measures of social and emotional growth, long recommended by critics of the test, as well as by the Head Start administration's own evaluation of the testing program.

"There have been tremendous gains when we were intentional," Mr. Wilkins said, adding that if the test is eliminated, "our ability to be informed will clearly be hampered."

Danielle Ewen, the director of child-care and early-education policy at the Washington-based Center on Law and Social Policy (CLASP), said Head Start staff members have felt pressure over such issues as how their NRS results will be used or if they are spending their funds appropriately.

"There is an environment of fear that has been created in many programs," she said. "They're worrying about those layers of accountability."

FUNDING SQUEEZE

Head Start also has been buffeted by a leveling-off of funding that the NHSA says has left some programs in dire circumstances.

A loss of transportation services, a cutback on meal portions, and the dropping of some comprehensive services are among the sacrifices administrators report having made over the past six years of flat funding at about $6.8 billion annually.

Mr. Bancroft said that at the centers in his area, which serve 1,700 3- and 4-year-olds, the family-support workers have had to increase their caseloads, and programs to train and employ parents have been reduced. Teacher salaries, typically below those of kindergarten teachers or of teachers in many school-based prekindergarten programs, have also been frozen.

At the Child Start site in Covina, the budget restrictions were felt when staff members working for the state received cost-of-living pay increases, but the Head Start employees did not.

"We're feeling it here on the front line," said Sandra Maldonado, an education coordinator for Options.

Mr. Wilkins doesn't disagree that Head Start agencies have had to tighten spending, and also said that some years saw large increases in funding for program improvements.

"This has been an opportunity for them to look at their decisions. Maybe they weren't as prudent as they should have been," he said.

Mr. Barnett, from NIEER, said that "the decline in real purchasing power" because of inflation in the past five years or so is probably even larger for Head Start programs than people think. He even speculates that the Bush administration is trying to "offload" the program in more subtle ways after the failure of its plan to convert the program to one funded by block grants. "Holding the Head Start budget down is certainly one way to give states more responsibility," he said.

An example from Alabama may back up his theory. State Rep. Laura Hall, a Democrat, said recently that she is preparing a bill that would shift $1 million from state education funds to Head Start programs. She said she hopes her legislation will be approved "especially in light of the fact that we do not have a statewide pre-K program." She added that "Head Start's 40 years of service" is one good reason for the state's support.

WORKING WITH THE COMMUNITY

Head Start programs also are grappling with how agencies now fit into a broader mix of publicly funded school-readiness programs.

"There are Head Starts that have been successful at integrating" children served by state preschool programs, Mr. Barnett said. "But there are others that have been very resistant and trying to do business as usual."

Head Start was a pioneer in reaching out to existing programs though state collaboration offices, which led to partnerships such as joint teacher-training workshops and cross-agency committees.

"That's the idea of Head Start—to be able to work with the community," said Cherry Chua, the program manager at Options.

When programs work together, they are often able to serve more children. Even before the large growth in state preschool programs, Head Start centers in the 1990s teamed up with federally subsidized child-care centers to provide longer hours to children whose mothers were working to meet the requirements of new welfare laws.

But working with public prekindergarten programs—which, in many states, allow Head Start providers to receive pre-K funding—raises different issues. Because state preschool programs tend to focus primarily on school-readiness skills, Head Start providers have expressed concern that other services such as health, nutrition, and family support, which are as much a part of the program as the educational component, will get pushed aside.

"They feel that they are the keepers of comprehensive care, and the kids who need it the most are going to get lost," said Helene Stebbins, an analyst of early-childhood-education policy who recently co-authored a paper with CLASP on Head Start and pre-K collaboration.

If a state's pre-K program serves children at the same family-income level as Head Start—which is 100 percent of the federal poverty level—a turf war over children can develop.

Tonya Russell, the director of the division of child care and early-childhood education in the Arkansas Department of Health and Human Services, said a combination of events in her state led many Head Start providers to blame pre-K for a decline in Head Start enrollment.

First, the state in 2005 increased funding for the Arkansas Better Chance pre-K program, which serves low-income families. Around the same time, the federal government began requiring monthly enrollment counts from Head Start agencies, which don't get paid for children who aren't attending.

Demographic shifts in areas long served by Head Start also have affected the program, which had its birth in the African-American community. The gentrification of some urban neighborhoods means that families eligible for the program have moved elsewhere, and some Head Start classrooms are left underenrolled, and perhaps unprepared to reach out to new immigrant groups.

"There are clearly enough eligible children across the country," Mr. Wilkins said, arguing that some grantees may need to "expand their ways" of attracting new families.

Preliminary results from a yet-to-be-released study by CLASP shows, for example, that even though Head Start programs might be adequately serving Spanish-speaking families, "they are not always providing meaningful access to non-English-speaking families" from other immigrant groups, such as Cambodians or Vietnamese.

THE RIGHT MIX

Some observers, who argue that children benefit from being in classrooms with peers from different socioeconomic levels, say they don't want to see Head Start continue to serve the poorest children while state preschool programs increasingly serve middle-class children.

"Segregating poor kids is not a good idea," Mr. Barnett said, adding that mixing Head Start programs with pre-K programs can benefit Head Start, "because people are willing to pay even more for poor kids in a program that is more universal."

But a combination of Head Start, pre-K, and child-care children in the same classroom or center can also mean a collision between different sets of standards over features such as class size, square-footage, nutrition, and other services.

"It took us two years to get pre-K teachers to brush [children's] teeth," Gina Ruther, the Head Start collaboration director in Illinois, said about a long-standing practice in Head Start. "They're still not doing home visits."

In that state, which has had prekindergarten for 20 years, a variety of arrangements exist. Some agencies serve Head Start and pre-K children in separate classrooms. Some children are counted in both programs, which might mean they receive more hours of class time. And in other local programs, classes are even team-taught by Head Start and pre-K teachers in order to meet the staff-credentialing requirements of both programs.

Mr. Bancroft said that partnerships between programs can be an "auditor's nightmare."

And Ms. Russell, in Arkansas, said some directors may worry about making mistakes that could show up on a monitoring report.

"There is a deep fear that [federal officials] will take our funding," she said, adding that staff members "just don't want a checkmark by their name."

Mr. Wilkins, however, said he has been "very clear that we're interested in collaboration" as long as it can be done without jeopardizing Head Start standards. He said he hopes Head Start providers feel supported by his office.

In Illinois, where Gov. Rod R. Blagojevich, a Democrat, has pledged to provide universal pre-K to both 3- and 4-year-olds, Ms. Ruther said she frequently tells grantees that they are in a "competitive arena" and that they need to promote what Head Start can offer that is different from what child-care and preschool programs provide.

"I try to remind people that, 'unless the feds do something to destroy you, Head Start provides families with some opportunities that the other two programs do not,'" she said. "As long as Head Start is still in the picture, things will be OK. These are just struggles to go through as we get there."

Bibliography

Books

Arrighi, Barbara. *Child Poverty in America Today*. Westport, Conn.: Praeger, 2007.

Barker, Robert L. *The Social Work Dictionary*. Silver Springs, Md.: NASW Press, 2003.

Barris, Fred R. *Locked in the Poorhouse: Cities, Race, and Poverty in the United States*. Lanham, Md.: Rowman & Littlefield Publishers, Inc., 1999.

Burger, William R. *Human Services in Contemporary America*. Florence, Ky.: Brooks/Cole, 2007.

Christ, Grace Hyslop. *Healing Children's Grief: Surviving a Parent's Death from Cancer*. New York: Oxford University Press, 2000.

Cochrane, Glynn. *Elephants and the Myth of Global Poverty*. Boston: Pearson, 2009.

Delgado, Melvin. *Social Work with Latinos: A Cultural Assets Paradigm*. New York: Oxford University Press, 2007.

Dubois, Brenda and Karla Krosgrud. *Social Work, an Empowering Profession*. Boston: Allyn & Bacon, 2005.

Edwards, John, et al., eds. *Ending Poverty in America: How To Restore the American Dream*. New York: New Press, 2007.

Ehrenreich, Barbara. *Bait and Switch: The (Futile) Pursuit of the American Dream*. New York: Henry Holt & Co., 2005.

Ehrenreich, Barbara. *Nickel and Dimed: On (Not) Getting by in America*. New York: Henry Holt & Co., 2008.

Eldersveld, Samuel James. *America: A Comparative Historical Study of Poverty in the United States and Western Europe*. Lanham, Md: Lexington Books, 2007.

Gibbs, L. E. *Evidence-Based Practice for the Helping Professions: A Practical Guide with Integrated Multimedia*. Pacific Grove, Calif.: Brooks/Cole-Thompson Learning, 2003.

Katz, M. *In the Shadow of the Poorhouse: A Social History of Welfare in America*. New York: Basic Books, Inc., 1996.

Lin, Ann Chih and David R. Harris. *The Colors of Poverty: Why Racial and Ethnic Disparities Persist*. New York: Russell Sage Foundation, 2008.

M. Rock, et al., eds. *Issues and Directions in Serving the Mentally Ill Offender in the Community*. New York: Springer, 2002.

Mink, Gwendolyn and Alice O'Connor. *Poverty in the United States: An Encyclopedia of History, Politics and Policy*. Oxford: ABC-CLIO, 2004.

Mui, A. C. and Shibusawa, T. *Asian American Elders in the Twenty-First Century: Key Indicators of Well-Being*. New York: Columbia University Press, 2008.

Novogratz, Jacqueline. *The Blue Sweater: Bridging the Gap Between Rich and Poor in an Interconnected World*. New York: Oxford: Rodale Press, Inc., 2009.

Payne, Ruby. *Framework for Understanding Poverty*. Highlands, Tex.: aha! Process, Inc., 2005.

Pogge, Thomas. *World Poverty and Human Rights*. Cambridge, Mass.: Polity Press, 2007.

Sachs, Jeffrey. *The End of Poverty: Economic Possibilities for Our Time*. New York: Penguin, 2006.

Shilper, David. *The Working Poor: Invisible America*. New York: Random House, Inc., 2005.

Soss, Joe, et. al. *Remaking America: Democracy and Public Policy in an Age of Inequality*. New York: Russell Sage Foundation, 2007.

Tileston, Donna Walker and Sandra K. Darling. *Closing the Poverty and Culture Gap: Strategies to Reach Every Student*. Thousand Oaks, Calif.: Corwin Press, 2009.

Williams, Rhonda Y. *The Politics of Public Housing: Black Women's Struggles Against Urban Inequality*. New York: Oxford University Press, 2004.

Winne, Mark. *Closing the Food Gap: Resetting the Table in the Land Of Plenty*. Boston: Beacon Press, 2008.

Yunus, Muhammad. *Banker to the Poor: Micro-Lending and the Battle Against World Poverty*. New York: PublicAffairs, 2003.

———. *Creating a World Without Poverty: Social Business and the Future of Capitalism*. New York: PublicAffairs, 2009.

Web sites

Readers seeking additional information pertaining to social services for the poor may wish to consult the following Web sites, all of which were operational as of this writing.

Children's Health Insurance Program (CHIP)

www.cms.hhs.gov/home/chip.asp

Created in 1997, the Children's Health Insurance Program (CHIP) is an initiative that enables states to secure matching funds from the federal government and provide health-care coverage for millions of uninsured young people. In 2009 President Barack Obama signed a bill reauthorizing the program, paving the way for the government to cover an estimated four million additional children. The CHIP Web site contains on overview of the program, as well as annual enrollment data and progress reports.

National Coalition for the Homeless

www.nationalhomeless.org/

The National Coalition for the Homeless has a simple mission: "to end homelessness." To that end, the agency works on both the local and national levels, organizing community projects and advocating for the types of broad policy changes needed to keep people from finding themselves on the street. The Web site includes news, research reports, and tips for getting involved, as well as information on the Bring America Home Act, a legislative initiative the agency is planning on reintroducing in Congress.

Supplemental Nutrition Assistance Program (SNAP)

www.fns.usda.gov/FSP

Formerly known as the Food Stamp Program, the Supplemental Nutrition Assistance Program (SNAP) helps feed more than 28 million Americans each month. Since October 1, 2008, when the new name took effect, the program has placed greater emphasis on encouraging healthy eating, and its prepaid cards can now be used only to purchase certain types of foods. The SNAP Web site includes information on eligibility and enrollment, as well as links to nutrition studies and program statistics.

U.S. Census Bureau: Poverty

www.census.gov/hhes/www/poverty/poverty.html

This Web site, maintained by the U.S. Census Bureau, provides a wealth of statistics concerning poverty in the United States. Detailed charts and tables illustrate how poverty rates have changed over time and continue to vary by region. The Web site also includes definitions of poverty-related terms and a Frequently Asked Questions section.

U.S. Department of Health and Human Services: Medicare

www.medicare.gov

The federal Medicare program covers nearly 40 million Americans, most over the age of 65. This Web site provides information regarding eligibility, enrollment, billing, and coverage. The site also provides an overview of the Medicare Prescription Drug Plan and offers searchable directories of doctors and healthcare providers.

The Urban Institute

www.urban.org

According to its mission statement, the Urban Institute "gathers data, conducts research, evaluates programs, offers technical assistance overseas, and educates Americans on social and economic issues—to foster sound public policy and effective government." The Web site features research papers on a variety of topics, including poverty/welfare, housing, and health/healthcare.

Additional Periodical Articles with Abstracts

More information about social services for the poor and related subjects can be found in the following articles. Readers interested in additional articles may consult the *Readers' Guide to Periodical Literature* and other H.W. Wilson publications.

The Missing Class. Maryann Cusimano Love. *America* p10 August 4–11, 2008.

President George W. Bush's opposition to the State Children's Health Insurance Program (SCHIP) is misplaced, Cusimano Love maintains. Since 1997, more than 6 million poor children have received health insurance through SCHIP. This important legislation offers states matching federal funding to cover uninsured children whose family income, although low, is higher than allowed to qualify for Medicaid. The law came up for renewal in fall 2007, and state governors, children's health advocates, the U.S. Conference of Catholic Bishops, Catholic Charities, the Catholic Health Association, and others all urged that the program be bolstered and expanded. President Bush twice vetoed the SCHIP legislation late in 2007, however, and Congress was narrowly unable to override the president's veto. Bush and some members of Congress argue that expanding SCHIP would extend coverage to middle-class and rich children, but the facts say otherwise.

City Officials Get a Feel For the Poor Life: Simulation Reverses Roles Of Public Assistance. *American City & County* pp18–19 January 2008.

In an interview, Dennis Campa, director of the San Antonio Department of Community Initiatives, discusses the aims of poverty simulations and the need for national policy changes to address poverty. The simulations involve government officials and community business leaders interacting with social service workers and managing finances in real-world scenarios to illustrate the complexity of the resources available to help people out of poverty. One of the problems identified is that going to one agency for help does not automatically provide the person with access to other federal assistance programs, to which they may be entitled, and that the personal information required to participate in these programs varies from state to state.

Raising the Spotlight on Affordable Housing. Ronald Roach. *Black Issues in Higher Education* pp24–26 December 19, 2002.

The work of scholars who study housing in the United States is informed by a deep-seated concern about housing conditions, Roach reports. Dr. Victoria M. Basolo, a professor of urban planning at the University of California-Irvine, and Dr. Michael P. Johnson at Carnegie Mellon University in Pittsburgh, Pennsylvania, are both motivated in their work by a desire to play a part in ensuring that all Americans have adequate housing. This is unsurprising, as the careers of scholars, such as Basolo and Johnson, who obtained their doctoral training during the 1990s coincided with what is widely regarded as one of the most acute housing crises in the United States since the late 1940s.

The Geography of Poverty. Dalton Conley. *Boston Review* p. 24–26 March/April 2007.

Social policy in the United States needs to focus on time and place rather than simply on money, the author argues. Significant new research has suggested that poverty is a reflection of economic segregation and the time bind faced by low-wage parents. Recent research on the geographical organization of poverty suggests that the main problem is social division. Time is also an integral part of how place affects poverty. To break the intergenerational cycle of poverty, it is necessary to address the issues of economic segregation and the family time crunch. Once this is understood, we can begin to rethink social policy in a more creative fashion.

Welfare Agenda. *The Christian Century* p5 September 19, 2006.

There have been both advantages and disadvantages to President Clinton's welfare reform law, enacted ten years ago, the writer maintains. Highly controversial at the time, the law set out time limits for receiving cash assistance and required welfare recipients, including single mothers with young children, to work. Even critics of welfare reform have had to concede that since 1996, the number of working mothers has fallen by 1.5 million, the median income of families on welfare has risen by several thousands of dollars, and welfare caseloads have been reduced by 60 percent. The concern that welfare-to-work would not help the least employable people—those without a high school diploma, with a disabled family member, or with a mental health or drug or alcohol problem—has been validated, however.

'Hunger' Not in USDA Lexicon. Aliya Sternstein. *CQ Weekly* p1240 May 12, 2008.

The U.S. Department of Agriculture does not quantify the number of hungry people in the nation, Sternstein reports, because the word "hunger" is basically banned by the government from the yearly surveys it uses to measure household access to food. Since 2006, following recommendations from a panel of the National Academies, the department decided that the condition measured in the food security survey is a household-level social and economic condition, not an individual-level physiological condition. The government now marks households along what it regards as a more accurate spectrum, ranging from "high food security" to "very low food security."

But It Works. Robert Cherry. *Commonweal* p7 September 26, 2008.

Many on the left believe Clinton-era welfare reform was mean-spirited and had grave implications for defenseless families, Cherry observes, but the reality is that President Clinton's "Make Work Pay" initiatives slashed poverty among single-mother households by 25 percent. Moreover, although their poverty rates rose slightly during the slow-growth period at the start of the present decade, those increases were much smaller than during previous slowdowns. Liberals were incensed by welfare reform mainly because it required recipients to engage in activities as a condition for eligibility, something they found particularly distasteful given America's history of racial discrimination. Fearful of "blaming the victim," some liberals have refused to accept that in order to break a destructive cycle, the welfare system had to require many recipients to modify their behavior.

The Untold Health Care Story: How They Crippled Medicare. Lilliam B. Rubin. *Dissent* pp51–54 Summer 2008.

The Bush administration's hostility to Medicare and Social Security has been well documented since the president took office, Rubin contends. However, although Bush lost the struggle to privatize Social Security, he has succeeded in pushing people into HMOs by increasing the monthly cost for Medicare and reducing services and payments to doctors, thus threatening the program's very existence. Unfortunately, the 2008 election campaign offers little hope of significant improvement in this health care crisis: candidates have shied away from proposing a government-sponsored, single-payer system similar to Medicare, a program that worked perfectly well until it was dismantled.

The Importance of Quality Early Childhood Education. Miquela Rivera. *The Education Digest* pp61-63 November 2008.

In this article, condensed from the March 24, 2008, issue of *The Hispanic Outlook in Higher Education*, Rivera argues that more Latino parents need to get their children into prekindergarten education. Early childhood education can level the academic playing field for Latino children entering school by supporting what parents are doing at home to teach their kids the skills required to succeed. However, only 20 percent of Latino children under the age of 5 are enrolled in preschool according to a report by the National Task Force on Early Childhood Education for Hispanics. Rivera discusses the importance of early childhood education programs and how they can involve Latinos.

The Poor Man's Burden. William Easterly. *Foreign Policy* pp76–81 January/February 2009.

Today's global economic disaster risks aborting the hopeful Revolution from Below, in which poor people took the initiative without experts' advice, Easterly reports. Eighty years ago, a depression changed the way the world thinks about poverty. It took decades for the world to recover and to realize that if people are given freedom, they will prosper. Today, in the wake of another massive collapse, the fear that shocked people into relying on government to fix poverty is spreading and threatening to undo many of the gains that have been made. The meltdown hit many poor nations from Asia to Africa to Latin America that are still experimenting with political and economic liberty but have yet to wholly embrace it and experience its benefits. For decades, these nations have struggled tremendously to realize the potential of individual creativity instead of the smothering hand of the state, and for a time it seemed that the power of individual liberty could be winning.

The Disappearance of Hunger in America. Patricia Allen. *Gastronomica* pp19–23 Summer 2007.

In November 2006, the U.S. Department of Agriculture (USDA) announced that it was eliminating the word "hunger" from its official assessment of food security in the United States, using the term "very low food security" instead, Allen notes. The media portrayed this decision as a political attempt to deflect attention from problem of hunger in an affluent society. In truth, the story is more complex and subtle than that. The statistical elimination of the term "hunger" does indeed harm hungry people and efforts to end that hunger. However, the term "food security" is also real and important, and it needs to be considered as a conceptual category in any discussion of the inequalities surrounding food.

The House That Government Built. Russell Roberts. *Hoover Digest* pp30-34 Winter 2009.

In this article, reprinted from the October 3, 2008, issue of the *Wall Street Journal*, Roberts contends that many overlook the role politicians and policy makers played in generating artificially elevated housing prices and mitigating the danger of highly risky assets. Starting in 1992, Congress pressured Fannie Mae and Freddie Mac to sell more mortgages to low- and moderate-income borrowers, allowing Congress and the White House to provide nonbudget finance for low-income housing in the short term, and the 1995 Community Reinvestment Act encouraged traditional banks to do the same thing—prompting an 80 percent rise in bank loans for low- and moderate-income families. Both Bill Clinton and George W. Bush, supported by Congress, hailed the historic growth in home ownership, but, as well as placing the whole financial system in danger, the hidden cost has been hundreds of billions of dollars channeled into the housing market rather than into more productive assets.

Lack Of Diversity Fuels Racism In Early Childhood, Study. *Jet* 24–25 October 9, 2006.

A study by researchers from the University of Maryland published in the September/ October issue of *Child Development* indicates that white children who attend mainly white schools are more likely to attribute negative intentions to black children than children enrolled in more diverse school settings, the writer reports. Melanie Killen, the study's coauthor, points out that these findings are quite novel because no previous research has explicitly examined the relationship between the ethnic diversity of children's social experiences and their attributions of intentions in familiar, everyday interracial situations.

Talking about Hunger in a Land of Plenty. Jennifer A. Weber. *Journal of the American Dietetic Association* pp804–07 June 2006.

According to Weber, the largest study to date of hunger in the United States has major implications for nutrition policy. In *Hunger in America 2006*, researchers for the food-bank network America's Second Harvest analyzed data from 52,000 face-to-face client interviews and 30,000 surveys of local charitable agencies conducted in 2004. The results reveal that food insecurity and hunger are prevalent among emergency food recipients; affect all ages, ethnicities, and locations; and impact the working poor and those with health problems, among others. One of the factors involved in the increased need for emergency food assistance is the failure of eligible participants to take part in national food-assistance programs. *Hunger in America 2006* also highlights the apparent overlapping of the incidence of food insecurity and obesity. The report represents another means by which dietitians can highlight the need for the services of food and nutrition professionals.

Deconcentrating Poverty With Housing Programs. Kirk McClure. *Journal of the American Planning Association* pp90–99, Winter 2008.

According to McClure, housing programs of the past have exacerbated the problems of concentrated poverty. Current housing programs serving very low-income households, including homebuyers as well as renters, should be examined to determine the extent to which they help households make entry into neighborhoods with low concentrations of poverty. The results of these examinations will help planners understand how well various approaches to resolving housing affordability problems can facilitate the poverty deconcentration process. Methods: Administrative data from the Department of Housing and Urban Development are used to assess the degree to which federal housing programs help low-income homebuyers and renters locate in neighborhoods where less than 10 percent of the population is below poverty. Results and conclusions: Subsidizing households ought to be more effective than subsidizing housing units at helping low-income households locate in low-poverty areas, and whether a household rents or buys should not matter to whether a program succeeds at deconcentration of the poor. Yet, analysis of national datasets across several housing programs finds neither of the previous propositions to be true.

Poverty Rate, Housing Costs Rise; Wages for Key Workers Unchanged. *Journal of Housing and Community Development* p16 November/December 2005.

In 2004, the official U.S. poverty rate rose to 12.7 percent, up from 12.5 percent the previous year, according to the 2004 report on income, poverty, and health insurance released by the Census Bureau on August 30, 2005, the writer observes. The report also indicated that the real median household income remained unchanged in real terms, a finding supported by the National Housing Conference's study, "Paycheck to Paycheck: Wages and the Cost of Housing in America." That study also revealed that although the median cost of a home rose 20 percent from fourth quarter 2003 to first quarter 2005, key workers' wages did not increase.

The Culture of Race, Class, and Poverty: The Emergence of a Cultural Discourse in Early Cold War Social Work (1946–1963). Laura Curran. *Journal of Sociology and Social Welfare* pp15–38 September 2003.

Through a primary source historical analysis, Curran discusses the emergence of a cultural discourse in the early Cold War (1946–1963) social work literature. It traces the evolution of social work's cultural narrative in relation to social scientific perspectives, changing race relations, and increasing welfare caseloads. Social work scholars originally employed their cultural discourse to account for racial and ethnic difference and eventually came to examine class and poverty from this viewpoint as well. This cultural framework wrestled with internal contradictions. It simultaneously celebrated and problematized cultural difference and foreshadowed both later twentieth century multiculturalism as well as neoconservative thought.

Schools Help Stop Hunger with Campus Kitchens Project. Donna L. Boss. *Nation's Restaurant News* p42 October 22, 2007.

Volunteers working for the Campus Kitchens Project, which was launched with the help of a grant from the Sodexho Foundation in 2001, have delivered more than a half-million meals to community members in need, Boss reports. The project combines the DC Central Kitchen model with a concept called Homerun that was established in 1999 by two Wake Forest University students to engage their peers in cooking and delivering dinners to community members. The success of Northwestern University's Campus Kitchens program is discussed.

Poverty Does Not Restrict a Student's Ability to Learn. Ruby K. Payne. *Phi Delta Kappan* pp371–72 January 2009.

The writer, who wrote *A Framework for Understanding Poverty* in the mid-1990s, discusses the criticism her book received and defends it, asserting that it emphasizes a belief in every individual's cognitive ability to succeed. The underlying theoretical construct for the work is situated learning, a concept put forward by Lave and Wenger of Columbia University in 1991. The aim of the book was to explain the situated-learning environment of generational, rather than situational, poverty and the bridges and strategies required for students to make successful transitions to the decontextualized environment of school. To survive poverty, one needs to be an incredible problem solver. The decontextualized environment of school means that students have to use an abstract representational system of knowledge that is learned and typically not available in the situated-learning environment of generational poverty.

Incentives Aren't Everything. Liam Julian. *Policy Review* pp91–96 December 2008/ January 2009.

According to Julian, the Republican Party's 1994 "Contract with America" may have been the inspiration behind Joseph V. Kennedy's decision to place a contract at the center of his new book, *Ending Poverty*. Kennedy's contract is one in which the author would replace the majority of the nation's extant entitlement programs. Kennedy believes that the United States can and must fight poverty but that a different approach should be adopted that requires the poor to meet specific obligations prior to receiving government assistance. The book's plan is doomed to fail, Julian asserts, because its premise rests on the supposition that poverty can be substantially decreased through wealth transfers (constructed as either incentive or reward) from financially secure Americans to poor ones. To understand poverty only as the absence of money is to misunderstand it completely.

How Does the SCHIP Exclusion Affect Health Insurance Coverage for Children of Low Income State Workers? Patricia Ketsche, et. al. *Public Personnel Management* pp313–25 Fall 2008.

A provision of the law that created the State Children's Health Insurance Program (SCHIP) to provide low cost coverage for moderate income children whose parents do not have employment-based coverage excludes children whose families are eligible for participation in a state employee health benefit plan from enrollment in the state's SCHIP program, the authors observe. This exclusion applies even when a child is not covered and would otherwise be eligible for SCHIP based on his or her family's income. This article presents an analysis of the implication of this policy on coverage among state employee dependents and the potential effect on these children. The writers found no evidence that low income children of state workers were disproportionately lacking coverage from 2002 to 2004, but rapidly increasing premiums in state benefit plans may portend problems for these children.

Changing Our Minds. Frances Moore Lappe. *Sojourners* pp30-31 September/October 2008.

Poverty can be eliminated in the United States, but only if the real obstacle is dealt with, Lappe argues. The main barrier to the eradication of poverty is not, nor has it ever been, a particular president or policy. The real obstacles are our ideas about poverty that rob citizens of the power to follow common sense and the innate need for fairness. For three decades, the proliferation of false and dangerous ideas has stunted our sense of the possible. Particularly deadly are the following misconceptions: we do not know how to end poverty, ending poverty would cost too much, ending poverty would require big government, society has to choose between equity and economic success, and equality is unnatural. Breaking free of these beliefs is what will start the end of poverty.

The Right Thing to Do. Jim Wallis and Jim Rice. *Sojourners* pp14–15+ September/October 2008.

Wallis and Rice interview Democratic Senator John Edwards, a candidate for the Democratic presidential nomination in 2008. He is currently director of the Center on Poverty, Work, and Opportunity at the University of North Carolina and chair of the Half in Ten Campaign, a movement to cut poverty by half within the next decade. In the interview, Edwards discusses such topics as the necessity to put poverty on the national agenda, the work of making alliances between anti-poverty campaigners and politicians, and the concrete steps American society needs to make in order to reduce poverty.

Index